The Myth of Media Violence

The Myth of
Media Violence
A Critical Introduction

David Trend

Blackwell
Publishing

BLACKWELL PUBLISHING
350 Main Street, Malden, MA 02148-5020, USA
9600 Garsington Road, Oxford OX4 2DQ, UK
550 Swanston Street, Carlton, Victoria 3053, Australia

First published 2007 by Blackwell Publishing Ltd

1   2007

Library of Congress Cataloging-in-Publication Data

Trend, David.
    The myth of media violence : a critical introduction / David Trend.
        p. cm.
    Includes index.
    ISBN-13: 978-1-4051-3383-8 (hardcover : alk. paper)
    ISBN-10: 1-4051-3383-X (hardcover : alk. paper)
    ISBN-13: 978-1-4051-3385-2 (pbk. : alk. paper)
    ISBN-10: 1-4051-3385-6 (pbk. : alk. paper)   1. Violence in mass media.   I. Title.

    P96.V5T74 2007
    303.6–dc22

                                                                        2006020377

A catalogue record for this title is available from the British Library.

Set in 10.5 on 13 pt Minion
by SNP Best-set Typesetter Ltd, Hong Kong
Printed and bound in Singapore
by Markono Print Media Pte Ltd

For further information on
Blackwell Publishing, visit our website:
www.blackwellpublishing.com

Contents

Introduction:
The Media Violence Tower
of Babble

In a now famous study conducted in the 1970s, a group of American researchers were convinced they'd come up with a perfect way to measure the effects of violent media.[1] They had decided to study teenage boys who lived in residential facilities and boarding schools where television viewing could be completely controlled. For a period of six weeks, half of the boys were permitted to watch only violent programs and the other half non-violent shows. Everyone expected the boys exposed to violence to become more aggressive and unruly, as similar studies of younger children had demonstrated. But the findings shocked everyone. As the weeks went by the boys watching the non-violent shows started fistfights and began vandalizing the schools. They disrupted classes and shouted expletives at teachers and each other, while the groups viewing the violent shows remained peaceful and studious, even more so than usual.

The researchers were baffled. Maybe the violent shows had helped their viewers blow off steam with some kind of cathartic effect. But past studies of catharsis had shown that it varied dramatically from individual to individual and never lasted very long. Soon more experts began examining the findings and eventually they came up with the answer. The group watching the non-violent programs had become angry because they had been denied their favorite shows (they were especially upset about *Batman*). Viewing enjoyment or unhappiness, it turned out, played a much greater role in the boys' behavior than the amount of violence they saw. In fact, the media violence seemed to have no effect whatsoever.

The point of this anecdote is not to suggest that media violence is harmless. My research over the past decade has convinced me that violent media cause plenty of harm. But the dangers are not always the ones that seem most obvious. The common-sense assumptions that one draws from watching a four-year-old boy throw a karate kick like a *Teenage Ninja*

Turtle do not necessarily apply to a teenager, an eight-year-old, or even another preschooler. Like the boys in the residence homes, people are affected by media in highly individualized ways. By the same token, the social factors underlying aggression and crime are influenced by far more than violent media. After decades of pronouncements by headline-hungry politicians and pop psychologists that social problems might be fixed with better TV viewing habits and fewer video games, the consensus of academics, educators, and policy makers has begun to shift in recent years to a more holistic consideration of violent media and violent people. This book is about that shift in thinking.

The Myth of Violence seeks to extend the conversation about media violence beyond simple arguments of condemnation or support. In questioning typical views of media violence, we'll view the topic in a broader context – taking into account the social, economic, and political factors that encourage and thrive upon violent entertainment. Also addressed will be the functions that violent stories perform in education, art, and historical accounts of violent occurrences in human history resulting from war, genocide, and natural catastrophe. In addition, the book examines the distinctly American style of much media violence. Historically the United States dominated global media production and was the source of most of the movies and television the world saw. The picture changed somewhat when multinational corporations began restructuring production and distribution in the 1980s and 1990s, but the influence of American-style TV and movie making has endured even in the face of burgeoning media industries in India, China, Japan, and Europe.

Beginning with a look at history, this book chronicles concerns about violence in the media that have accompanied the development of new communication media from the printing press to the internet. *The Myth of Media Violence* then charts the ways that different stakeholders in the media violence debate – audiences, producers, and academics – often have viewed the topic in mutually exclusive, one-dimensional terms. This book discusses why, in the face of so many efforts to curb the proliferation of violent material, media violence continues to escalate in new and more potent forms. *The Myth of Media Violence* addresses the ways this ubiquitous culture of violence contributes to broader social anxieties over harm and catastrophe. The book then analyzes the forces that encourage these anxieties – exacerbated in the post-9/11 era – and how these forces mitigate against a progressive and democratic society. Finally, the book closes with a chapter about why media violence exists and how we can learn to deal with it.

The common-sense assumption that depictions of violence promote deviant behaviors predates the invention of film and television. Victorian-era street theater and penny novels were thought to encourage misbehavior among the working poor, especially young men in urban areas. Indeed, some accounts of the media violence debate date to Aristotle. For this reason, any serious examination of media violence needs to begin by examining historical continuities in the public concern over violent expression, while also noting the unique ways that different media convey violence. Questions need to be asked about why, after decades of public debate, policy analysis, and academic scrutiny, the discourse on media violence remains riven with inconsistency. While certain groups of researchers (primarily in the social sciences) continue to assert that violence in media is bad, firm conclusions about why it is bad have failed to materialize. In part, this results from difficulties in consistently defining "media violence."

What is Media Violence?

The media violence question has resisted resolution in part because the topic is so hard to define. At first, most people have no trouble calling to mind a violent image from a cop show, horror movie, or video game. But is media violence simply a matter of depicting physical harm? Does it need to be aggressive or intentional? What about accidents or natural disasters? Does psychological torment count? What about verbal or implied violence? Are there degrees of violence? Is justified violence better for viewers than the gratuitous variety? What about humorous violence? Sports? How about violent documentaries? Or the nightly news?

Part of the problem is that violent representations are so deeply ingrained in our culture. For centuries violence has been an important element of storytelling, and violent themes appear in the classical mythology of many nations, masterpieces of literature and art, folklore and fairy tales, opera, and theater. Religious texts like the Bible and the Koran use episodes of violence to dramatize moral lessons and to teach people to care for each other. Fairy tales warn children about the violent consequences of not behaving as instructed by adults. Great paintings and public monuments record human history with depictions of violence. And what about violence today? Eliminating violence from home entertainment has become a lot more feasible now that TVs are built with V-chips. But what would that mean? Getting rid of offerings like *Fear Factor* and *The Amityville Horror* (2005) on the basis of violence alone would also rule out important films like *Saving Private Ryan* (1998), *Schindler's List* (1993), or *Hotel Rwanda*

(2004) – not to mention popular children's films from *The Lion King* (1994) to *The Shaggy Dog* (2006).

The ubiquity of violent representations has made them a part of everyday life, and their volume keeps growing. Pick up any newspaper or turn on the TV and you will find either violent imagery or a story about violent media. Like the war on poverty, the war on drugs, and the war on terrorism, campaigns to stem the tide of media violence have failed. The most systematic quantitative studies of media violence are those conducted about television, where the frequency of violent incidents can be assessed relative to total programming. Some of the more alarmist voices in the media violence field have claimed a young person will witness 200,000 simulated violent acts and 16,000 dramatized murders by the age of 18.[2]

Researchers studying media violence have attempted to arrive at "scientific" definitions in efforts to measure media violence. In the 1960s and 1970s this often meant something as simple as counting the number of times a character threw a punch or shot a gun, with incidents on *Colombo*, *Star Trek*, and *Get Smart* all given the same weight. No distinctions were drawn between realism, fantasy, and comedy until the 1980s, when some researchers began considering the plausibility or effects of violent incidents, as well as psychological aggression. Efforts to define media violence reached a watershed moment in the mid-1990s, when a consortium of research universities conducted the National Television Violence Study (NTVS), analyzing over 10,000 hours of broadcast material. Studying 23 channels, the NTVS found 18,000 violent acts for each week of programs it analyzed – or 6.5 incidents per channel per hour. The study determined that the average adult watched four hours of television each day.[3] Children watched three hours a day.[4] These patterns persist. Violence is seen on TV by people of all ages. In addition to the violence regularly seen in television dramas, sports, and Saturday morning cartoons, news coverage of war, terrorism, and crime has increased the sense of immediacy and realism in televisual violence. This has been amplified by the rise of reality-based programs and the generalized message that the world is becoming a more dangerous place.

The NTVS was the first study of its size to argue the importance of context in considering violent material, making the startling statement that "not all portrayals of violence are the same."[5] It makes a difference, the NTVS stated, whether the violence is presented graphically on-screen or simply implied. It matters what type of character commits the violence, why, and with what kind of consequence. Is the violence committed by a hero or "good guy"? Is the action justified or rewarded? Does the violence cause pain and suffering? Or perhaps it seems to have no effect at all, as in many cartoons and comedy programs. Do we sympathize with the victim? Or not? Finally, who is the audience for the violence? The NTVS argued forcefully that not all people react to violence in the same way. The point is that not all media violence is created equal. But rarely are these many distinctions and nuances mentioned in public debates over these issues.

The potency of violent depictions in movies is continually enhanced by computer-generated special effects. This not only makes for more spectacular pyrotechnics. It also has blurred the line between reality and fantasy as never before. The incidence of gore may not have increased over that brought to movies by the "new violence" directors of the 1990s like Abel Ferrara, Oliver Stone, and Quentin Tarantino, but the formal means by which violence could be visualized and thus imagined grew with advances in technology. Science fiction films like *Revenge of the Sith* (2005) and *X-Men: The Last Stand* (2006) introduce new kinds of blasters, phasers, and aliens as horror films like *Saw III* (2006), *Slither* (2006), and *Ghost Rider* (2007) suggest that vampires and other killers can materialize just about anytime from thin air. A spate of war films like *Troy* (2004), *Flyboys* (2006), and *Pathfinder* (2006) use digital technology to bring thousands of combatants to the screen, as have fantasy movies like the *Lord of the Rings* trilogy (2000–4). Popular imports like *Ichi the Killer* (2002), *The Grudge 2* (2006), and *Tsotsi* (2006) have vividly portrayed mass murder and suicide – often focusing on teenage victims – as computer effects have allowed martial-arts films like *Hero* (2004), *House of Flying Daggers* (2005), and *Fearless* (2006) to launch physical combat into supernatural dimensions. Some analysts assert that the aesthetics of media violence simply satisfies existing audience desires for violent fare. In the 1960s, anthropologist Karl Lorenz argued that primitive instincts in people make them seek out stimulating experiences.[6] George Gerbner has concluded in what he terms "cultivation theory" that viewers become acclimated to ever more potent forms of violent representation that raise their thresholds for such material and heighten the level of intensity of programs they seek.[7] Dolf Zillmann has made similar assertions in articles and research papers. It's worth noting in this context that some researchers have argued that media violence is less appealing to audiences than TV formats like comedy or game shows.

Computer games are fast advancing to become the leading source of violent entertainment as market penetration in 2005 surpassed 50 percent of the US population.[8] In 2002, people around the world spent $31 billion on computer games versus $14 billion on movies.[9] The Entertainment Software Association asserts that adult game players (39 percent of whom are women) spend 7.5 hours per week engaged in the activity and that 84 percent of people playing computer games are over the age of 18.[10] Some in the media violence community believe that the interactive character of computer games makes them a more influential "teacher" of aggressive behavior than movies or television, although such assertions have yet to be proven conclusively by scientific research. Regardless of its effects, computer gaming has become an enormous business – with the budgets of game development and promotion now surpassing that of many feature films. This is hardly surprising in light of the fact that popular games like *Grand Theft Auto: San Andreas* (2004) and *Halo 2* (2004) both sold over 2.4 million copies (retailing at $49.95) on their first day of release, putting them on an economic par with the most successful Hollywood movies. With 957,000 units sold, the number one game of 2005 was "World of Warcraft," which placed participants in an environment where they hunted, shot, and blasted hundreds of other players.[11]

A Cacophony of Voices

Further complicating the media violence debate are the vast differences among the participants – and their varied ways of thinking and talking about this complex issue. Parents may approach media violence quite differently from professors who study the subject or the industry professionals who produce it. Then factor in variances in parents' religious beliefs and level of education, the professors' academic discipline and definition of "truth," and the industry professionals' medium and intended audience. At best this is a recipe for misunderstanding and frustration. In the highly charged and often emotionally laden discourse of media violence it also has been a formula for distortion and dishonesty.

Put another way, debates over media violence can be viewed as symptoms of larger concerns over social values, behaviors, and the role communications technologies play in people's lives. Because media violence has prompted concern among such a vast and diverse set of groups, it has generated a fragmented array of questions, accusations, hypotheses, and answers, many of which address important aspects of the media violence debate, but few that adequately consider its complexities, interrelationships, and contradictions.

One can identify perspectives in this fragmented media discussion from six groups, each with its own agenda and ways of talking about the issue. Given their varying reasons for looking at media violence and the different ways they perceive and describe the issue, these groups create a contemporary "tower of babble" that fails to adequately address media violence and undermines ways to cope with it. They are *consumers, producers, advocates, experts, politicians,* and *reporters.*

Consumers. This group includes parents, kids, adults, and people with whom they interact daily like teachers, counselors, physicians, and clergy. Its agenda is to find coherent information about the potential risks of media violence and easy-to-understand ways to do something about it – like monitoring kids' viewing habits, using the V-chip, Cybersitter, or Net Nanny.

Producers. Media is a business. The primary agenda in the entertainment and news industries is to attract audiences. Profit making supersedes concerns over ideology, ethics, or the social consequences of media. This perspective generally defends practices in the interest of free speech and a free market, or by asserting that media violence simply reflects today's society.

Advocates. Foundations, advocacy groups, and non-profit organizations like the Children's Defense Fund, the Christian Coalition, and the American Medical Association articulate concerns of consumers in the interest of bringing attention to issues and recommending action or legislation. At times this rhetoric can betray an ideological bias or political agenda.

Experts. Writers and researchers are often cited in the media violence debate with the belief that such "experts" provide objective and unbiased perspectives. But the very nature of expertise is specialization. Hence, experts bring their own perspectives, fields of interest, and varying levels of quality and veracity.

Politicians. Lawmakers, commissions, and candidates for office have clear stakes in appearing responsive to constituents in their defense of public safety and "family values." Often responding to the latest shocking movie or school tragedy, politicians favor hyperbole over sober rhetoric and quick fixes over long-term efforts.

Reporters. Newspapers, magazines, TV, and internet journalists need to convert complex events into easily digested reports. As a consequence reporters often condense, exaggerate, or simply distort research findings, frequently embellishing them with opportunistic commentary from public officials or the anguished reactions of families victimized by violence.

This jumble of competing claims and arguments is enough to confuse even the most discerning reader. The result is a kind of intellectual paralysis that subverts efforts to help the situation. Clearly ways are needed to reconcile the contradictions among these sympathetic, yet methodologically incompatible, groups. This work will involve a synthesis of positions that requires parties with disparate perspectives to come together and listen to each other's views. Otherwise the discussion will remain mired in polemics and bickering. As one veteran of the field recently wrote, "Although scientific researchers have produced a strong body of evidence demonstrating that exposure to media violence harms society, the evidence has never been translated into practical and accessible ideas."[12]

The absence of practical plans to address violence is becoming all the more frustrating with the recognition that the perceived problem seems to be escalating. Recent advances in digital-effects technologies, the exploding popularity of computer games, and growing consolidation of profit-driven media conglomerates are pushing violence with unprecedented ferocity. Perhaps not so coincidentally, this is occurring at a historical moment when catastrophes in real life are often barely distinguishable from those created for the screen. The public appetite for violent imagery across a broad spectrum of formats has firmly established violence as a production staple. Besides appealing to the broadest domestic audience demographics, the visual quality of violent fare makes it easily marketable in non-English speaking "after-markets" around the globe. Moreover, movies heavy with digital special effects are now becoming cheap to make. This financial incentive not only drives the selection of what films get made, it increasingly factors in how movies initially are conceived. The same holds true with the burgeoning computer game market, which repeats narrow formulas of pursuit and assault decorated with digital weaponry, gore, and sound. The Kaiser Family Foundation reported in 1999 that most homes with children had video game hardware.[13] Many people argue that the interactive character of games makes them far more potent as "teaching machines" than other media. Such general perceptions, especially as the risks pertain to young children, have been articulated in literature reviews by Lillian Bensley and Juliet Van Eenwyk and by Mark Griffiths.[14] This is why it is so important to look at the economic underpinnings of these industries and the way market forces interact with public demand for violent entertainment on a global scale. Examining these issues helps explain the growing supply of such material and why efforts to stem the tide of violent material have failed.

Then one has to ask why we haven't gotten further in efforts to do something about the overwhelming onslaught of violent imagery. Concern is growing that the escalation in the volume and intensity of representational violence is occurring at a time when the general level of public fear is also rising. As movies, television, and games deliver fictional accounts of terror and disaster, the news media serve up accounts of murder, road rage, gang warfare, workplace violence, drug trafficking, internet porn, plane wrecks, killer moms, and medical malpractice. News – or the news that gets reported – is increasingly driven by spectacle. This is especially the case on television, where network journalism has been losing out to splashier fare from Fox, CNN, MSNBC, and other cable providers. As a consequence, television news is far more likely to feature readily visualized stories of conflict or crime over less telegenic issues like health care or child poverty. The result is a public obsessed about risk and catastrophe far in excess of any real danger. Statistics reveal that there was no epidemic of child abductions last year and that gun-toting teens are not invading the nation's schools.[15] But what continues to occur to a disturbing degree is what communications specialist George Gerbner has termed the "mean world syndrome," as audiences become convinced over time that life is more dangerous.[16] Not only does this lead to heightened public anxiety, but it also makes recognition less likely of actual dangers to people's lives – like drunk drivers or fast-food burgers. It makes people likely to support reactionary public policies advancing quick fixes for fear rather than those that address the complexity of community concerns. In this way the mean-world effect is an impediment to healthy civic discourse.

Until fairly recently much television, movies, and computer games that featured hyperviolence conveyed the impression that harm strikes outside of suburban America. Violence mostly happens to "someone else." It tells audiences, often inaccurately, that brutality and suffering exist in some faraway place, but not at home. This is what has afforded recent sniper attacks, child abductions, and office bombings such emotionalism: the recognition that bad things don't only happen to other people. Yet contrary to speculation following the events of September 11, 2001 that a fearful public would avoid movies and television about "homeland" atrocities, the opposite has occurred. Fed a daily diet of sensationalized news stories and color-coded terrorist attack warnings, the public craving for tales of war and apocalypse has grown, as evidenced by the success of films like *Collateral Damage* (2002), *United 93* (2006), and *World Trade Center* (2006). Connections to the 9/11 events can be quite explicit. Currently, leading computer games among US teenagers include "Splinter Cell," about hidden terrorist cohorts, and "Counterstrike," in which players choose roles as terrorists or counterterrorists.

As these narratives circulate within the US, they are exported around the globe by an American media industry that dominates worldwide film and television production. Violent media spectacles enhanced by sophisticated digital effects appeal to the widest demographics and translate most easily across age and language barriers. The profitability of violence drives movie production, television programming, and most computer games, as media corporations compete in developing the most engaging strains of hyperviolence. The violent images that the US sells around the world portray the US and its people as the center of the universe. These productions also tell other nations that America is a forceful, deadly, and unbeatable adversary. This is one of the reasons why the US military often supports the production of movies and television that glorify its war-making abilities.

Media violence isn't going to disappear and most current efforts to stop it are unlikely to succeed. Like displays of material excess and gratuitous sex, violence exists within a commercial structure predicated on a powerful system of fantasies. Whether or not we like to admit it, these fantasies accrue their appeal and popularity because they are linked to people's deepest desires and fears. Clearly these impulses might be expressed in more productive – or more creative – ways. The issue isn't so much that there is too much violence circulating in the media. It is that the violence we see is so narrowly conceived and conveyed. Big media's need for big audiences and shareholder returns has created a very small view of the world. What we need are more diverse and expansive representations of life with all of its tragedies and violent episodes – as well as its joys and inspirations. Certainly, efforts on a personal level can be made to choose entertainment with discretion, to supervise viewing by children, and to not support offensive material. In institutional terms, important work is being done through media education programs and consumer efforts to hold the media industry to higher standards. But a "just say no" approach to media violence is no more a solution for consumers than new regimes of government censorship are for producers. We need a more open and representative media system that affords variety in production and genuine choice in consumption. The growing popularity of interactive programming available through the internet and digital search-and-record technologies has revived the promise of media diversity once anticipated from cable television.

This book will discuss the ubiquity of media violence and the hysterical popular discourse it has generated. The issue has been fodder for headline-hungry politicians and religious extremists pandering to the fears of a public often misinformed by distorted news reports and opinion pieces masquerading as fact. Not that intellectuals have done much better. Given the breadth and complexity of the issue, academics working in a variety of disciplines have generated a myriad of contradictory findings and theories. Where one stands in the media violence issue depends very much on what questions are asked and who asks them. Largely lacking in the debate are voices that attempt to combine perspectives from areas like social sciences, film studies, cultural studies, and political economy. Yet unless one considers the media violence question broadly in this way, only a partial understanding of the topic will result.

1

We Like to Watch: A Brief History of Media Violence

Media violence is one of the most widely discussed yet least understood issues of our time. The ubiquity of violent imagery in everyday life makes it a topic about which everyone has an opinion. Yet the fractured and contradictory character of the public debate on media violence offers little insight. Instead the discussion degenerates into arguments between those who fear and those who relish such material. Lost in these discussions are considerations of why violent representations are so common and how they satisfy certain audience desires. Rather than blaming the entertainment industry for producing violent television, movies, and games, it is important to consider why demand is so strong for them. The answer is that violence works. Like racism and sexism, the desire for violent representations is not a deviation from a social norm. It is the norm.

Media Violence in Historical Perspective

Violence has always figured prominently in storytelling. Violent imagery has been around since hunters began scratching accounts of their exploits on the walls of caves. Whether or not one believes that violent behavior is innate in human beings, violence has always played a major role in storytelling. Artifacts of Egyptian, Sumerian, Minoan, and Babylonian peoples all depict violent events, as do classical works of the ancient Greeks written 3,000 years ago. All rely on violence to propel their narratives. Homer's *Iliad* (c.760 BC) relentlessly recounts military conflict, assassination, mass execution, sexual assault, and natural disaster. The same holds true for the *Odyssey* (c.680 BC), Hesiod's *Theogony* (c.700 BC), Aeschylus's *Oresteia* (c.458 BC), Sophocles' *Oedipus the King* (c.428 BC), and Thucydides' *History of the Peloponnesian War* (c.424–404 BC). The books of the Old Testament, written during the same period, are filled with accounts of genocide, war, human sacrifice, and, of course, various plagues. And as Mel Gibson so eloquently reminded moviegoers with his hugely successful film, *The Passion of the Christ* (2004), the biggest story of the New Testament culminates in rioting, ritual torture, and public execution. Perhaps more to the point, these grizzly stories have been repeated for centuries to children and adults alike as important works of history and religion.

The pattern continues in the centuries to follow, suggesting that violence is deeply embedded in the type of stories Western civilization tells itself. Literary works of the Middle ages like Dante's *Inferno* (1302) and Chaucer's *Canterbury Tales* (1386–1400) were riddled with detailed descriptions of violent assault and death. The best-known plays of William Shakespeare, including *Hamlet* (1607), *Julius Caesar* (1600), *Macbeth* (1606), *Othello* (1605), and *Romeo and Juliet* (1595) relied heavily on patricide, fratricide, suicide, and plain old murder to drive their plots. These works by Shakespeare were in their day the cultural equivalent to *Desperate Housewives* and *CSI*. Everybody saw them, from the illiterate "groundlings" who sat on the floor of the public theater to university-educated elites or those who might attend plays in special performances of the plays at Queen Elizabeth I's court.

The printing press enabled dissemination of these and other works beyond the stage. Gutenberg's invention of movable type in 1452 and the subsequent development of vellum paper meant that by the mid-1500s over 1,000 print shops were operating in Europe. As printing improved over the next century, "true crime" books began recounting criminal acts and the brutal punishments that awaited those apprehended. The books satisfied a hunger for gore and provided warnings for potential offenders. It's probably worth mentioning that during this era public executions took place regularly in most European countries, attracting huge audiences for violent displays of state authority. By the mid-eighteenth century the modern novel was born with the publication of Samuel Richardson's *Pamela* (1741) and with it came the first public outcries over the effects of media. Richardson's story of a virtuous servant girl preyed upon by an unscrupulous seducer was excoriated in tracts circulated throughout London condemning it for "lewdness" and for assaulting "Principles of Virtue."[1]

These concerns over the degrading effects of gritty entertainment grew more pronounced in the decades that followed. The introduction of plate lithography in 1801 made possible the mass production of books, pamphlets, and broadsides. In the United States, *The National Police Gazette*, first published in 1833, arose to satisfy the public hunger for stories of violent crime. History has demonstrated that periodic "moral panics" over media seem to parallel the development of new communications technologies and the social changes they enable. The Gutenberg press and the lithography process made possible dramatic leaps in the dissemination of written works. Both technologies allowed ordinary people access to what had formerly been available only to the privileged.

And it made the elites nervous. This was certainly true in the mid-1800s, when commentators began to link social problems of the industrial era to emerging forms of popular media, often evoking images of an idealized past free of such difficulty. Modernity had created a new working class of factory laborers often living in overcrowded urban tenements and hungry for the diversion provided by dime novels, newspapers, and vaudeville-type shows pandering to tastes for lust and violence. An English critic writing in 1851 described "one powerful agent for depraving the boyish classes of our population in our towns and cities is to be found in the cheap concerts, shows and theatres" that become "training schools of the coarsest and most open vice and filthiness."[2] According to Graham Murdock, such sentiments typified a bourgeois fear of a growing working class of adolescent "hooligans" in need of policing. Like current formulations of an "epidemic" of violence in the media from which children need inoculation, nineteenth-century media critics like Frank Lydston wrote of a "psychic contagion in certain books that is as definite and disastrous as that of the plague. The germs of mental ill health are as potent in their way and . . . as far reaching in evil effects as syphilis or leprosy."[3]

Nineteenth-century modernism grew fond of expressing social concern in scientific terms, with medical metaphors deployed in many contexts. Drawing on terminology of germ theory and epidemiology, writers discussing poverty spoke of "infections," "contagions," and "plague spots" within impoverished communities.[4] To Herbert Spencer, such sickness was a necessary part of social evolution:

> Having, by unwise institutions brought into existence large numbers who are unadapted to the requirements of social life, and are consequently sources of misery to themselves and others, we cannot repress and gradually diminish this body of relatively worthless people without inflicting much pain. Evil has been done and the penalty must be paid. Cure can only come through affliction.[5]

The invention of photography in the mid-1800s made the production of moving pictures possible by the end of the century. Violence was the centerpiece of early movies. Thomas Edison demonstrated the new technology in 1895 with his Kinetoscope film *The Execution of Mary, Queen of Scots*, a 30-second clip of a beheading. Movies of boxing matches proved to be a sensation. The immediate success of *The Corbett–Fitzsimmons Fight* (1896) gave it the dubious distinction of being one of the first films to evoke the ire of anti-media violence critics, a sentiment that led to a ban on prizefighting movies in 1912. Like today's effects-laden action films, graphic depictions in movies like Sigmund Lubin's *Chinese Massacring Christians* (1900) or Georges Méliès's *The Last Days of Anne Boleyn* (1905) were used to help show off the features of the moving image. Early movies were especially popular among the new immigrant populations emerging in urban centers. The visual language of film made proficiency in English irrelevant to these audiences.

Soon local lawmakers and social reformers grew concerned over the perceived risks of exposing the ethnic-minority working class and the young to such fare. When New York City Mayor George McClennan ordered moving-picture exhibition licenses to be revoked in 1908, a group of theater companies (including Biograph, Lowe, Edison, and Pathé), founded the National Board of Review (NBR). As the entertainment industry would do again in later decades, this gesture of self-regulation served to preempt government intervention in movie content. The NBR passed moral judgments on films, failing those that glorified crime or that it believed presented excessive "suffering, brutality, vulgarity, or violence."[6] Approved films often ran the legend "Passed by the National Board of Review" in their title sequences. The regulation of movies took place in the context of more generalized concerns over public morality and the productivity of the national workforce. Such thinking led to the 1919 passage of the Eighteenth Amendment prohibiting the manufacture and sale of alcohol, which remained in effect until repealed by Congress in 1933.

Regulation Efforts

In 1922 film production companies formed their own regulatory organization, the Motion Picture Producers and Distributors of America (MPPDA), which established standards of appropriate content. The MPPDA was led famously by Will Hays, who for two decades was recognized by the American public as the nation's "movie czar." The MPPDA efforts led to the establishment of the film industry's "Production Code," which codified content guidelines. Recognizing that movies "may be directly responsible for spiritual or moral progress, for higher types of social life, and for much correct thinking," the Production Code, which remained a governing force in movie making from 1930 to 1958, deemed inappropriate depictions of such practices as murder, "brutal killing," safecracking, the "dynamiting of trains," adultery, "lustful kissing," or miscegenation.[7] Bolstering these views were the findings of the influential Payne Fund Studies conducted in the late 1920s. Surveying the attitudes of students and young adult office workers, the Payne Fund concluded that "motion pictures are a genuine educational institution; not educational in the restricted and conventional sense . . . but educational in the truer sense of actually introducing (viewers) to a type of life which has immediate, practical, and momentous significance."[8] Although conducted with research subjects described as "adolescents," the study framed its findings on "the great influence of motion pictures on the play of children" as "a source for considerable imitation," characterizing children as "blank slates."[9] This extrapolation from the observation of children would become a template for most discussions of media violence for the rest of the century. Together with the Production Code, the Payne Fund Studies succeeded in sanitizing most motion picture production through the 1960s. The only movies that escaped such regulation of violence were World War II-era newsreels.

With the end of World War II public concern in the US shifted to domestic well-being. The newly emergent suburban middle class sought safety and often settled for conformity, while seeking to avoid threats of any kind. Attention focused on the perceived dangers posed by undisciplined young people, immigrant populations, communists, and the growing popularity of violent western and crime movies. A senate investigation launched by Estes Kefauver in 1950 concluded that comic books contributed to juvenile crime rates. Not unlike the infamous McCarthy Hearings of the same period persecuting perceived communists, the Kefauver proceedings sought to prove a connection between crime and immigrant groups, primarily focusing on the Italian mafia. Within a few years other media became targets of the Kefauver Committee by association, with the genre of teenage film blamed for making young people insensitive to crime, death, and pain. Prompted again to act in the interest of avoiding government regulation, the film industry in 1956 enacted a voluntary moratorium on the production of "juvenile delinquency" films like *The Wild One* (1953) and *Rebel without a Cause* (1955).

Things changed significantly in the 1960s. With the dissolution of the Hollywood studio system, the structural underpinning of industry self-regulation loosened. At the same time, the mood of social activism in the US emboldened filmmakers to think more independently. In particular the Vietnam War fostered a national conversation about the nature of aggression and conflict. The result was more violence on the screen. Movies either reveled in gore or used it to awaken audiences to consequences of aggression in films ranging from *Psycho* (1960) and *The Misfits* (1961) to *Bonnie and Clyde* (1967) and *Night of the Living Dead* (1968). Director Sam Peckinpah asserted that he lengthened the gunfight scenes in his western *The Wild Bunch* (1968) to impress audiences with the true horror of combat. But what really worried people was sex. Films like *Who's Afraid of Virginia Woolf?* and *Blow Up* (both 1966) pushed the envelope of what could be said and shown with explicit language and graphic footage. In 1968, newly installed president of the Motion Picture Association of America Jack Valenti announced implementation of the voluntary movie-rating system that would evolve into the G, PG, PG-13, R, and NC-17 system in place today.

The media again came under public scrutiny in the "culture wars" of the 1980s. Entertainment and the arts were blamed, along with schools, for weakening intellectual and moral fiber in the US and other nations. But Americans led the way in calling for a return to traditional values and education. During the Reagan administration the Office of the Attorney General was charged with policing culture through the infamous Meese Commission on Pornography convened from 1985 to 1986. Although the Meese Commission succeeded in drawing public attention to pornography, it did little to change the sex industry and had no legislative impact whatsoever.

Changes did occur in the music industry, which was transformed in the 1980s by two phenomena: MTV and hip-hop. Vividly brought to life in music videos, explicit song lyrics provided the impetus for the formation of the Parents Music Resource Center (PMRC), organized in 1985 by Tipper Gore (spouse of former vice-president Al Gore) and Susan Baker (wife of former Reagan White House Chief of Staff James Baker). The group came into being, as the story goes, when the Gore family (including 12-year-old Karinna) heard the word "masturbation" while listening to Prince's *Purple Rain* album. Gore quickly assembled sixteen other "Washington wives" and drew up a list of the "Filthy Fifteen" for presentation to a congress. Asserting that Prince's "Darling Nikki" and Madonna's "Dress You Up" were responsible for rising rape and suicide rates among those between the ages of 16 and 24, the PMRC garnered so much legislative support so quickly that the recording industry voluntarily developed its now well-known "Parental Advisory" labels before any laws were ever written. The television industry similarly initiated a voluntary program-labeling system in anticipation of the 1990 Television Violence Act requiring it to do so. Responding to criticism that the television labeling system was ineffective, letter coding was added in 1997 to indicate contents with "coarse language, sex, violence, and sexual dialogue."[10]

By the late 1990s a broad-based consensus had solidified around the common-sense notion that violence in the media must produce violence at home and in the streets. This consensus was supported primarily by a number of widely publicized studies conducted within a subdiscipline of psychological research. Arguably the most frequently cited summary document is the 1999 *American Academy of Pediatrics and the American Academy of Child and Adolescent Psychiatry's Joint Statement on the Impact of Entertainment Violence on Children.*[11] The report asserts that over 1000 studies "point overwhelmingly to a causal connection between media violence and aggressive behavior in some children."[12] A meta-analysis, the joint statement draws upon prior studies rather than research conducted by either professional organization. A similar statement issued in 1993 from the American Psychological Association said that "there is no doubt that higher levels of viewing violence are correlated with increased acceptance of aggressive attitudes and increased aggressive behavior."[13] It's important to note that the APA did not state that violent media *cause* aggression, only that a correlation was identified. In other words, aggressive individuals may consume violent media without the violence being the reason for the aggression. Due to the ambiguity in these findings, US Surgeon General David Sachter would not list exposure to violent media as a cause of behavioral violence among young people, observing that it is "extremely difficult to distinguish between the relatively small long-term effects of exposure to media violence and those of other influences."[14]

Continued arguments that television carried too much sex and violence led to the provision requiring television sets made after 2000 to contain the V-chip, an electronic component allowing the selective blocking of programs with certain ratings. Ironically, as the number of TVs equipped with the protective technology has grown, most parents have no idea how the V-chip works, or even know that their TV set contains one. In a survey by the Kaiser Family Foundation, only 15 percent of parents reported using the V-chip. Many respondents (39 percent) didn't realize that their new TV sets were equipped with a V-chip, while others (20 percent) knew they had a V-chip, but didn't use it. More to the point, even if parents knew how to use it, for the V-chip to be effective in blocking programming, TV networks consistently would need to identify program content with labels shown at the beginning of programs (such as "V" for violence, "L" for harsh language, "S" for sexual material, and "D" for sexual dialogue). Such labels do not appear on all shows. The story is the same for internet use.

While most parents have heard about the widely publicized dangers of internet porn and sexual predators lurking in chat rooms, most parents either do not have or do not know if they have software on their computers that monitors where children go online or with whom they interact.[15] Finally, in a survey sure to drive some parents crazy, it was discovered that 50 percent of young people use the internet while also watching television.[16]

In the years since 2000 – and especially since 9/11 – the media violence debate momentarily lost the frenzy of concern seen in the 1990s. A growing number of researchers have recanted dire predictions of the negative effects of violent movies and computer games, as scholars from the humanities and social sciences have added more nuance and complexity to the discussion. In 2001, a group of media scholars asked the American Academy of Pediatrics and the American Academy of Child and Adolescent Psychiatry to reconsider their joint policy statement issued that year on media violence because of its "many misstatements about social-science research on media effects." The group of scholars, which included such notable intellectuals as Jib Fowles, Henry Giroux, Henry Jenkins, Vivian Sobchack, and Pulitzer Prize laureate Richard Rhodes, cited the statement's factual inaccuracies and its "overall distortions and failure to acknowledge many serious questions about the interpretation of media violence studies."[17] Subsequently a research subculture began developing around the examination of positive aspects of media and game culture. A notable example of this scholarship is represented in James Gee's *What Video Games Have to Teach Us About Literacy and Learning*.[18] In this work Gee takes a cautious look at the neurological processing skills that game technologies help develop, without leaping to the conclusions of more hyperbolic writers in this area like Steven Johnson, author of *Everything Bad is Good for You*.[19]

Historical Continuities in Media Violence Debates

Viewed over time, distinct patterns have emerged in the way media violence has been perceived and acted upon. These patterns are associated with new media technologies, public concerns over populations perceived to be "at risk," beliefs that media violence causes other social problems, the engagement of consumer anxieties by public figures, and strategies to avoid regulation. New media technologies often democratize communication by making information more widely available to the average person. In doing so these technologies can enable larger changes in society. This certainly was the case when the printing press allowed the dissemination of written texts beyond a privileged elite in the fifteenth and sixteenth centuries. The mass distribution of ideas and news helped enable the establishment of modern nation-states no longer defined solely by geographical borders set by mountains and bodies of water. The printing press also disseminated to common audiences the earthy stories and plays of the era. New lithographic processes in the nineteenth century made possible the dime novel and the first real public uproar about the corrupting influence of violent media.

Another wave of public concern followed the invention of moving pictures in the late nineteenth century. The rapid adoption of cable TV in the 1980s brought music videos – and the subject matter of popular music – to the attention of an anxious generation of parents. A similar explosion in computer game and internet use in the 1990s triggered another groundswell of concern over violent media. In each of these instances, it was not so much the technology that caused the real concern as the "vulnerable" populations discovering new access to information. "The pattern is always the same," says literary historian Harold Schechter; "a new medium of mass entertainment comes along aimed at – or embraced primarily by – kids and the working class. Very quickly, high minded reformers begin to denounce it as a sign of social decay, a corrupter of the young, a threat to the very existence of civilization as we know it."[20]

Representations of violence have remained popular as the lived experience of physical violence continues to decline in the Western world – or, to be precise, the more privileged parts of that world. As crime has declined and medical services have improved through the last two centuries, the majority of citizens in the US and other G8 nations increasingly found suffering and violence to be things far removed from daily life. Historian Vicki Goldberg points out that in the 1800s disease, malnutrition, and famine reminded people daily of the limits of their mortality. "Over time, social, religious, and medical changes made dying and death gradually withdraw from view; by mid-nineteenth century they became virtually invisible in most large metropolitan centers, especially in America and England."[21] Oddly, this coincided with a long increase in images of death, driven in part by the development of photographic and publishing technologies. Much has been said in recent decades about the replacement of "real" experience with a world of images. Michel Foucault, among others, has written of the human need to repeatedly envision what is feared as a means of coping with the attendant anxieties. As violence is condemned, it is endlessly reproduced throughout public culture.[22]

Public concern over perceived "at-risk" populations accompanied each wave of violent material. In what would become a familiar refrain, the moral campaigners of the 1800s grew concerned about working-class youth and new immigrant groups swelling the populations of new urban centers. Similar worries returned when moving pictures came along, accompanied by new anxieties over the influence of media on children. It should be remembered that in the early decades of the twentieth century people didn't possess modern understandings of child development that explain how young children view and comprehend very differently from grown-ups. In the decades from 1900 to 1930, children were viewed simply as small adults distinguished from their elders only by the fact that their minds were "unmarked slates." In this view it seemed perfectly reasonable that life as a factory worker might begin at age seven or eight with the appropriate training. It also seemed logical to assume that if children imitated what they saw in movies, unsophisticated adults would do likewise. The Payne Fund Studies of the 1920s used a combination of questionnaires and the "direct observation of children" in reaching its conclusions about the dangers of violent movies to adults.[23] The belief that children's reactions to media could provide insights about adult responses persisted for decades and it remains the basis for much "common-sense" thinking about media violence today.

But children aren't the only worry. While most people claim that media violence has no effect on their behavior, they can easily list groups they think are at risk. During the nineteenth century this meant working-class youth. In the early days of movies the concern shifted to new immigrant groups. Then the fear was juvenile delinquency and gangs. In the 1980s, worries about urban crime triggered controversies over lyrics of rap groups. Consider the case of the album "Straight Outta Compton" (1989) by rap group Niggaz With Attitude, which featured the songs *Cop Killer* and *Fuck tha Police*. Not only was the hugely successful album banned from record stores across the nation and excoriated on the floors of Congress, but shortly after its release it also triggered a much publicized FBI investigation on the grounds that it encouraged "violence against and disrespect for the law enforcement officer."[24] The assumption was that the recording would drive young people to assault police, even though not a single such incident was ever reported. Terrance McDermott has pointed out the prevalence of violent references in American popular music, such as Johnny Cash's *Cocaine Blues*: "Early one morning while makin' the rounds, I took a shot of cocaine and shot my baby down. I shot her down and I went to bed. I stuck that lovin' forty-four beneath my head."[25] Yet no public outcry was ever voiced for songs like Cash's or for movies and television programs from *The Godfather* to *The Sopranos*. Hysteria about media violence is selective. It has less to do with the authorship or content of the material than with the imagined audience. Presumably the teenage consumers of hip-hop culture will be incapable of resisting its violent allure, while people who buy country music or view mafia movies will remain unmoved.

Beliefs that media violence causes other social problems have been the basis of much controversy over the years. From nineteenth-century worries that dime novels would enflame street hooligans, to turn-of-the-century concerns over the ill effects of moving pictures, to assumptions in the 1920s and 1930s that gangster movies were behind rising crime rates, to investigations in the 1950s into suspected mafia ties to the comic book industry – the media has been a scapegoat, a place for the Western world to focus its deepest anxieties and fears. When rap music arrived it was blamed for gang violence. With every violent incident in a school another warning is issued about antisocial music lyrics or overly violent movies. When public attention shifted in the late 1990s to computer games and the internet, the rhetoric about violence became increasingly shrill – as evidenced in the best-selling book *Stop Teaching Our Kids to Kill*, by David Grossman and Gloria DeGaetano.[26] This work asserted that while terrible, the "passive" consumption of violence in TV and movie viewing is less dangerous than the "active" participation in electronic games. The book based its arguments on the presumably solid conclusions of what it termed "thousands of existing studies" (3,500 to be exact) proving its claims. The book's real novelty – and what makes it valuable in understanding the popular discourse of media violence – was the way it clung to the unsubstantiated belief of negative effects in arguing against trends that point the opposite way. For example, despite the statistical decrease in overall crime and youth crime in recent decades, Grossman and DeGaetano said that a hidden momentum persists from earlier years. Contrary to reports from police and the FBI of fewer arrests, they asserted that rising incarceration rates prove their point. Ironically, rising incarceration rates in California, New York, and many other states were attributed by many experts to exactly the kind of paranoia that books like *Stop Teaching Our Kids to Kill* generates – resulting in reactionary legislation like Megan's Law and three-strike sentencing mandates. Identifying himself as a professor of "killogogy" for the Marines, Grossman argued that the US military currently uses "first-person shooter" computer games like *Doom* and *Quake* to condition infantry soldiers to shoot reflexively at human targets, successfully reversing a phenomenon discovered during World War II in which nearly 85 percent of soldiers were found to be intentionally missing those they were instructed to kill. "Across America we are reaping the bitter harvest of this 'training,' as ever more kids shoot their girlfriends or the teachers," Grossman writes.[27]

With each school shooting or similar tragedy certain public figures have seized upon the opportunity to rattle popular anxieties. The temptation to cash in on a flurry of public emotion has proven too tempting for many political leaders. A vocal Senate critic of media violence, Senator Joseph Lieberman has described what he terms "a culture of carnage" fostered by the industry. Parents feel "locked in a losing competition with the culture to raise our children," Lieberman has said.[28] The Columbine High School shootings in Colorado illustrated that the media violence children see "has become part of a toxic mix that has actually now turned some of them into killers."[29] In the same context Senator Bob Dole exclaimed that "the mainstreaming of deviancy must come to an end, but it will only stop when the leaders of the entertainment industry recognize and shoulder their responsibility."[30] Bill Clinton stated that computer games tell kids to "get in touch with your gun-toting, cold-blooded murdering side."[31] These same tendencies to scapegoat media violence with a "politics of substitution" appeared repeatedly in the uproars against media in the 1930s, 1950s, and 1980s. Speaking of this historical trend, respected communications scholar Todd Gitlin has said, "the campaign against the devil's images threads throughout the history of middle-class reform movements."[32] On a similar note former FTC Chairman Marvin Pitofsky has stated, "there is no cause-and-effect relationship between violent content and violent actions of teenagers, but that won't stop politicians from exploiting the cause-and-effect relationship between popular opinion and the ballot box."[33]

Industry strategies to avoid regulation have been remarkably consistent. In nearly every instance of public outrage, entertainment producers have headed off government intervention with promises of voluntary self-regulation. This began in 1908 with the movie industry's National Board of Review that would inspect new films for inappropriate content. The 1930 MPPDA Production Code put in place guidelines that regulated movies for 30 years. Both contemporary movie ratings and parental advisory labels on music and video games were developed before lawmakers could stipulate content restrictions. This has been a clever ploy. The labeling strategy launched in the 1960s has let entertainment producers off the hook by shifting responsibility to retailers and consumers. It has meant that profitability is one of few factors determining content. This affects more than the amount of violence and sex in movies. It has contributed to an incremental narrowing of entertainment genres and formats in the interest of predictable returns for shareholders.

Media Hysteria and the Culture of Fear

Much as they crave violent media, people still worry about media's effects. This concern is driven by two main factors, the first of which is the short-term hysteria periodically ignited by sensationalized incidents of violence. The second and more vexing factor is the generalized culture of fear perpetuated by a hodge-podge of child advocates, political opportunists, ratings-hungry broadcasters, and academic attention-seekers. The short-term hysteria has been fed by a relatively small number of tragic and highly publicized shootings by teenagers and children. In March 2005, a 16-year-old boy killed his grandfather then went to school and shot a teacher, a security guard, five students, and finally himself, leaving a total of 10 dead. In September 2004, a 15-year-old Argentinian killed three students near Buenos Aires. In September 2003, a teenager killed two students at a high school in Cold Springs, Minnesota. In April 2002, a 19-year-old murdered 13 teachers, two students, and a police officer at a secondary school in Erfurt, Germany. In May 2001, a 15-year-old boy killed two students and injured 13 at a school in Santee, California. In May 2000 a 13-year-old murdered a teacher at a school in Florida. One of the most publicized of these events occurred in April 1999, when two students used guns and bombs to kill 13 people at Columbine High School in Littleton, Colorado. Earlier high-visibility killings by teenagers took place in Arkansas, Kentucky, Mississippi, Washington, and in nations including the Netherlands, Germany, Sweden, and Yemen.

Accounts of these shootings have offered a variety of explanations of why they occurred. All of the assailants were boys with ready access to guns. Most of the boys had become alienated from school. And like most teenagers the boys had consumed copious amounts of violent media. Many analysts of the shootings see media as a background issue at best. But for others the resemblance between fact and fiction is just too close. The film *Basketball Diaries* (1995) is often cited in this context. In *Basketball Diaries* students imagine going on a shooting spree exactly like Columbine. Although more than a decade has passed since the film's release, anti-violence groups still cite the movie as a threat. Without any actual evidence to support it, the similarity between an unsettling fictional story and a very real tragedy is simply too compelling to resist. This is how public anxieties are mapped onto the media violence debate – by inference, association, and circumstance rather than reasoned analysis.

It's a vicious cycle by which violent entertainment and news create a reasonable public concern that is brought to the level of complaint by advocacy groups and academics. This is answered by the hysteria of producers, politicians, and reporters who battle over the issues in the arena of public media. The inevitable result is the further perception of a problem and a heightened concern that starts the cycle again. Every time a tragedy occurs, the same litany of accusation and blame follows in what some commentators term a "moral panic" or a "politics of substitution" that will give the irrational act of violence a logical explanation. The blame is placed on video games, or gangster rap, or drugs, or Satan, or the guns themselves, or perhaps an affinity for bowling, as Michael Moore suggested in his film about the shootings.[34]

The Media Hysteria Cycle

Parents and community-minded adults are understandably concerned about violent media. Entertainment media rely on the dramatic tension and titillation of the danger of violence to sustain the attention of the viewers. Movie and television producers often defend their artistic decisions with the argument that violence has been an essential component in storytelling throughout history. The excess of such material in the commercial marketplace proves this point, they claim. Apologists for media violence in academic circles similarly assert that viewers derive a sense of pleasure, satisfaction, or relief from viewing such material – with theories, surveys, and studies to bolster their claims. On the nonfiction side, it's no secret that newspapers and network news departments face unprecedented pressure from new forms of competition from cable and internet news providers. This has created a trend toward shorter and more sensation-driven reporting delivered without expensive and time-consuming analysis. Segments about violent crime, calamity, or disaster fit the bill perfectly, especially if they can be padded with wire news service embellishment or material from a network feed. All of this contributes to a "culture of fear" that leaves viewers looking for a voice to articulate their responses and an authority to calm their anxieties.

Advocacy groups and academics next enter the picture giving voice and urgency to community concerns over violent fare. These include the Pew Research Center for the People and the Press, the American Medical Association (AMA), the Benton Foundation, the American Academy of Pediatrics (AAP), the American Academy of Child and Adolescent Psychiatry (AACAP), religious groups like the American Family Association and the Christian Coalition, and single-issue organizations like Media Watch and Morality in Media. While occasionally sponsoring their own studies, most of these groups rely on researchers and media "experts" who can provide research and opinion that confirm negative conclusions about the media. An academic subculture has developed in response to the huge demand for such damning proof, along with a mythology inflating its findings.

Politicians and media producers are drawn into the public spotlight by reporters and the sheer pressure of the advocacy process. George Bush decried the "damage that comes from the incessant, repetitive, mindless violence and irresponsible conduct that permeates our media all the time." Hillary Clinton has entered the fray, proclaiming that kids are either wasting their time in front of the tube or playing games like *Grand Theft Auto* – a computer game which, according to Clinton, tells teenagers "to have sex with prostitutes and then kill them."[35] Meanwhile, many conservatives see violent media as but one more indicator of moral decline. Congress reacted by requiring the labeling of television programs and the inclusion of the "V-chip" in TVs. Movie, music, and game producers have adopted voluntary labeling. The internet remains unregulated and the violence continues – in the advertisements, toys, comics, amusement parks, cereal boxes, bubble-gum cards, and the rest of the flotsam and jetsam that comprise the universe of kid culture. Thus, despite the identification and labeling of media violence, the overall level of cultural violence remains unchanged.

The Win-Win Situation

The stakes for the players in the media violence debate often go unexamined. Who gains and who loses from media violence and the publicity it generates? Obviously, the news and entertainment industries think they need violence to capture audiences and believe they are justified in using it. But others benefit as well. Media violence is such an easy target for critics. It's everywhere and something everyone understands, or think they understand. For politicians, public health groups, and advocates of family values, media violence is a convenient target. It simply must be a factor in the spread of crime, delinquency, and moral decay. To Senator Lieberman America's children now live in "a culture of carnage" in which events like the Columbine shootings demonstrate that media violence "has become part of a toxic mix that has actually now turned some of them into killers."[36] This kind of rhetoric is great for galvanizing electoral support for legislators and for generating contributions to advocacy groups. Sociologist Howard Becker coined the term "moral entrepreneur" to describe public figures who seize upon such cultural issues for their own gain.[37] Other commentators take the argument a step further in suggesting that by focusing on such easy targets as sex and violence in the media, public officials divert attention from more complex social problems like poverty and inequality. Convinced that *The Texas Chainsaw Massacre: The Beginning* (2006), *Wind Chill* (2007), and *Ghost Rider* (2007) will make them unsafe in their own homes, voters are less likely to worry about other families who can't afford groceries. This "politics of substitution" has a serious secondary effect as well in contributing to widely held beliefs that the world is becoming more dangerous. Inundated by violent fictional programming and news stories about conflicts in faraway lands, people are also told by elected officials and community leaders that potential harm abounds in their "real" lives. No wonder so many people argue that they need to possess guns as a basic right. These beliefs have grown substantially in the years since the terrorist attacks of September 11, 2001.

The Facts about Crime and Violence

Two factual questions need to be addressed directly in the media violence debate: the amount of actual crime and violent behavior in society, and the degree to which consumption of violent media can be linked to crime and violence. According to the US Department of Justice, violent crimes have decreased in the last decade – after remaining somewhat constant for the prior 20 years.[38] Between 1993 and 2003 the number of "violent victimizations" per 1,000 people nationwide dropped by half – falling from 49 to 22 after hovering between 40 and 50 for the preceding two decades. According to the FBI, there were just under 1.4 million crimes of murder, manslaughter, rape, and robbery in 2005, 3 percent fewer than in 2004.[39] Aggravated assaults, which make up two-thirds of all violent crimes, have dropped for ten straight years. The Justice Department says that the homicide rate nearly doubled from the mid-1960s to the late 1970s. In 1980, it peaked at 10.2 per 100,000 population and subsequently fell off to 8.0 per 100,000 in 1984. It rose again in the late 1980s and early 1990s to another peak in 1991 of 9.8 per 100,000. From 1992 to 2000, the rate declined sharply. Since then, the rate has been stable.[40]

School violence also declined. Contrary to impressions fostered by media coverage of school shootings, the victimization rate for students at school fell from 1992 to 2002, according to the National Center for Education Statistics.[41] Violent incidents at schools during 2002 totaled 88,000 or approximately 20 percent of the 389,000 overall reports of violence against young people during the year. The percentage of students who reported being afraid of being attacked at school or on the way home decreased from 12 percent to 6 percent. The number of students bringing weapons to school decreased during the decade from 12 to 6 percent. Teachers became safer as well, although in recent years instructors in urban environments reported a higher incidence of assault (5 percent) than those in rural schools (3 percent).

What about the effects of media violence? For much of the 1980s and 1990s the US was awash with what appeared to be a solid academic consensus about the cause-and-effect relationship between media violence and real-world violence. As late as 2000, the AMA, the APA, and the AACAP issued a joint statement famously stating that "well over 1,000 studies" had proven a direct link between violent images and juvenile aggression. Harvard psychologist Steven Pinker wrote that it had become the overwhelming belief "among conservative politicians and liberal health professionals alike . . . that violence in the media is a major cause of American violent crime."[42] Then the case began to unravel. The scholarly consensus about media violence was in fact a fabrication. Although its findings received little news coverage, a large study of television program content conducted by several universities – the National Television Violence Study (NTVS) – concluded in 1997 that TV was less likely to provoke people into violent behavior than it was to convince them that violence is a normal way of solving problems. The NTVS also warned that exposure to violence in the media may lead people to believe that violence is everywhere and that they should be afraid.[43]

Accounts of the thousands of conclusive studies (some reports claimed as many as 2,000–3,000) turned out to be based on counts of *references* to negative findings rather than individual studies themselves.[44] The real number was less than 200. Then experts started coming forward. There never had been a consensus among psychologists, criminologists, or media researchers. Scholars in the media violence field like Jonathan Freedman, Melanie Moore, and Steven Pinker began asserting that the edifice of scientific proof about media violence was a myth. The body of research conducted was in fact inconclusive, contradictory, and often flawed – in some cases even fabricated. As the evidence against the media violence myth began to mount, more luminaries in the field began to backtrack. Following a blistering critique in 2000 of the anti-media violence camp by Pulitzer-winning journalist Richard Rhodes, two of the most famous figures in the social science side of the debate – L. Rowell Huesmann and Leonard Eron – conceded that "Nowhere have we ever indicated that media violence is the only or even a major cause of violence among youth."[45] Instead, they said, media violence is a marginal "risk factor" relevant to less than 10 percent of crime.

When the scientific edifice began to crack, other long-ignored opinions began to emerge from people who study mass media, audience behavior, patterns of consumption, and the culture of young people. Many of these scholars had for decades been arguing that the viewing public had a lot more sense than many experts thought. The baby-boom generation raised on television – now in its forties and fifties – had a healthy skepticism about what it watched and had parented an even more media-literate generation of computer-savvy offspring. These audiences were not the passive "couch potatoes" satirized by intellectuals in the 1960s and 1970s, but a highly diversified constellation of consumers whose viewing options came not from the local movie theater and a few major networks but from a dizzying array of thousands of programming choices from cable, satellite, DVD, computer game, and internet providers. The media had fostered a form of literacy.

2

Watching Doesn't Make Us Violent:
Assessing the Research on Media Violence

Media violence remains widely perceived as a problem. Despite contradictions in media violence research and a growing academic consensus against alarmist claims, concerns over media violence retain their hold on public opinion. The problem is that objective scholarship on media violence often is either misunderstood or mischaracterized by people with other interests or fears. The study of media violence is complicated and defining the issue is just one of the difficulties. Figuring out how to examine it is another. This chapter will examine the ways media violence has been studied and the fact that while it may not directly cause people to fight or commit crimes, it does promote an acceptance of violence as a fact of life and a generalized fear that comes from thinking the world is a violent place. And it does plenty of other harmful things – like supporting a superficial entertainment market, the commercialization of children's culture, and damaging stereotypes of women, men, and minorities.

Despite calls for abstinence, surveillance, V-chips, and ever more intrusive forms of regulation, the entertainment industry continues to produce an expanding array of apocalyptic movie spectacles, grizzly news reports, and hyperrealistic simulation games. And audiences continue to consume them. This means that media violence is big money for the entertainment industry. It also means that research about media violence has become a huge academic subculture. Driven by groups like the American Medical Association, the National Parent Teacher Association, and the US Congress, the stakes for media violence are high and research support is plentiful. The academic players in the media violence debate approach the issue from wildly varying perspectives. As a result little coherence or agreement has emerged after decades of study. Methodological differences and disciplinary divides have produced a myriad of conflicting studies and books with titles like *Is Media Violence a Problem?*, *Ill Effects: The Media Violence*

Debate, The Case for Television Violence, Endangered Minds, and *Mommy, I'm Scared: How TV and Movies Frighten Children and What We Can Do to Protect Them.*[1] The lack of clarity in the media violence discussion results from the inability of academic disciplines to talk with each other. Media violence literature has become a jumble of unrelated excursions into empirical science, narrative analysis, and communication studies.

The Biology of Violence

When discussing theories of media violence it's useful to consider human violence itself, which is a topic fraught with debate. After all, if one believes that violence is a normal part of human nature, violent media may not make much of a difference. On the other hand, if violent behavior is something people learn, media might have a huge influence. Biological explanations for violent behavior held sway through the nineteenth century. It was thought that human beings were simply another species, and that among animals violence was a natural element of evolution. Many historians trace the roots of this thinking to Thomas Malthus, who published his theory of "natural selection" in a 1798 article about English cities entitled "Essay on the Principle of Population."[2] Malthus observed that in nature plants and animals produce far more offspring than can survive, and that humanity too is capable of overproducing if left unchecked. Malthus concluded that unless family size was regulated, humanity's misery of famine would become globally epidemic and eventually destroy civilization. This explanation that poverty and famine were natural outcomes of population growth and food supply was not popular among social reformers who believed that with proper institutions, such ills could be eradicated. But Malthus had a tremendous influence on later thinkers.

Building on the work of Malthus, Charles Darwin concluded that nature had a way of dealing with overpopulation, writing that, through "continued observation of the habits of animals and plants, it at once struck me that under certain circumstances favorable variations would tend to be preserved, and unfavorable ones to be destroyed."[3] In his book *The Origin of Species,* Darwin argued that through a process of "natural selection" stronger animals would prevail over weaker ones.[4] Violent behavior among animals was a natural part of hunting and self-protection. It enabled the "survival of the fittest" and by extension the improvement of the species. Darwin's theories of natural selection laid the groundwork for the field of genetics used today to help scientists develop new strains of crops and predict inherited medical problems.

"Natural" explanations for violent behavior got more complicated after 1900. Scientists observed the territorial instincts of animals and the way many species acted out dominant and submissive social behaviors. These "social Darwinists" argued that natural selection explained and justified human competition and free-market economics. In more extreme applications, some social Darwinists asserted that natural selection accounted for social hierarchies based on social class, gender, and race – and that efforts to redress inequities constituted improper interventions against nature.

Immigration, urbanization, and industrialization in the early decades of the twentieth century pushed intellectuals to study human behavior and social organization. Carl Jung and Sigmund Freud became famous for their theories about the workings of the human mind. In different ways, both men asserted that the craving for violence was an inherent part of human nature. Jung suggested that destructive "shadow" archetypes live in people's unconscious minds. When the shadow archetypes are brought to light and recognized – often through violent representations – they evoke a moral encounter that ultimately leaves the individual edified and more thoroughly human.[5] Freud considered symbolic violence an important component of development, originating as an inherent drive manifest in Oedipal and castration complexes. Freud thought that people could keep their violent drives in check most of the time, but that they could lose control when frustrated. Sometimes people refer to this as the "drive" or "frustration–aggression" theory of violence. Like Jung, Freud believed that human beings mature through their struggles with the violence inside them and that stories offer an important way to address this struggle.[6] These ideas remained influential through much of the twentieth century as various thinkers developed theories about how to help people who couldn't control their drives. By the 1960s many scientists believed that people were born with a "threshold for violence" that could be measured with tests and strengthened with medical treatment.[7] Doctors might use shock treatments or brain surgery, as dramatized in Ken Kesey's book and movie *One Flew over the Cuckoo's Nest*.[8]

Not everyone in the 1960s agreed with these beliefs in humankind's "natural" tendencies toward violence or the related drive theories. Anthropologists like Ashley Montague had begun to assert that people learned to become violent through their upbringing and social experiences. Montague attracted a great deal of attention by arguing that theories of evolution and natural selection had been used to provide excuses for human violence. People needed to take responsibility for violence, Montagu said. It's probably no coincidence that this was also a time when anti-war movements were growing around the world, but especially in the United States and France – the two nations most involved in efforts to stop interventions in Vietnam. Philosopher Hannah Arendt became a voice for pacifists of the era in her classic book *On Violence*, published in 1969.[9] Arendt argued that people were not ruled by violent instincts because human beings possessed the capacity of reason. Arendt also contradicted the popular belief that the anger produced by poverty and other social inequities naturally resulted in violence.

More recently, psychologist Dolf Zillmann has written about the history of biological explanations for human aggression – the belief that primitive, animalistic inclinations drive people to vicarious experiences of hunting and fighting. This unfortunate "pseudo explanation," as Zillmann terms it, helps perpetuate the incorrect belief that violence is a natural consequence of anger, and that aggression is a natural part of life. The related category of "protective vigilance" asserts that people are driven to seek violent imagery by a need to continually monitor their environments to keep them safe. "The sharing of information about danger used to be adaptive," Zillmann writes, adding that in today's world "It would seem to be the rare exception that media reports of violent danger have such a utility. It is more likely that unrepresentative, danger-exaggerating incidents make the news and create maladaptive anxieties."[10] Then there are the categories of "moral monitoring" and "justice through violence," both of which ascribe ethical analysis to the viewing of media violence. Horror films have been the object of dozens of additional theories that circulate in the literature of media from the "social fear" hypothesis put forward by Stephen King (horror films "often serve as an extraordinary barometer of those things which trouble the night thoughts of a whole society") to the "snuggle theory" ("one source of attraction to horror films is that these films provide the occasion for men and women to practice and fortify traditional gender roles").[11]

The Psychology of Violence

If violence can't be explained by human nature, where does it come from? Most psychologists will say that it is what is learned or acquired through experiences that causes people to become violent. There also are theories about violence that result from mental illness. Given the extent to which violence pervades human history and culture it isn't surprising that people believe it's a natural fact of life. From early childhood, youngsters are exposed to violence in fairy tales, religion, toys, and the media. Violence pervades the literature and history studied in school as well as the games and sports engaged in on the playground. Mental heath professionals now agree that most human beings acquire violent behavior through either cognitive or emotional processes.

In cognitive terms, people learn to act aggressively by seeing other people react in violent ways. Being hit by a parent or seeing others start fights, a child comes to think this is normal behavior. Children (and adults) also learn violence from role models they seek to emulate. And of course environment plays a big role. Family, peers, social institutions, and culture all contribute to attitudes and beliefs that sanction violence. Within this context media violence plays a role in aggressive behavior, but not much more than a supporting role. The reason a person commits a murder or a robbery is far more powerful and complex than the entertainment coming from the TV set.

Emotion is important too. Angry feelings can and do cause people to attack or fight back. Sometimes people commit violence simply because they've become aroused or excited – as sometimes happens to police chasing suspects or to crowds at sporting events. In such instances the aggressors didn't plan to hurt anyone, but got carried away by the "excitation transfer" of the moment. In other instances, violence can come from deep inside someone who has been hurt in the past. Repressed feelings can slip out and result in violent behavior from an event too painful to consciously think about. Or people might be numbed by trauma so severely that they "dissociate" – or fail to realize what they are doing in committing violent acts. In a similar way, people with mental illnesses can become violent without being completely responsible for their actions. In such cases, chemical imbalances in the brains of sociopaths, schizophrenics, and people with bipolar disorders or other kinds of delusional episodes can lapse into violent behavior.

The idea that violent media deliver a cathartic effect has been largely disproved in research studies.[12] Media do not enable viewers to become purged of anxieties or aggression. Yet the common-sense assumption persists that emotional shock might somehow relieve people of tension or pent-up hostility. The catharsis hypothesis has a very long history, first appearing in the writings of Aristotle, who wrote that drama might purge audiences of feelings of anxiety or sorrow. Psychoanalytic theory bolstered twentieth-century beliefs in catharsis in suggesting that heightened aggressive drives need forms of release. But only one or two studies have ever supported the notion that viewing movies or television might yield a cathartic release of aggression. And both the 1971 Feshbach and Singer research and the 1991 study by Liebert, Sobol, and Davidson have been discredited as methodologically flawed.[13] Writing in 2001 of the catharsis studies, Bushman and Huesmann stated "there is not a shred of convincing scientific data to support this theory." An extended discussion of these issues appears in the summation of catharsis in Nancy Signorielli's *Violence in the Media: A Reference Handbook.*[14] This is not to say that violent media fail to deliver an emotional jolt, however. Many people enjoy the transitory shock or fear that such programming provides, often resolved through a restorative act of justice or other form of narrative closure. In a similar fashion, violent events in movies or television undoubtedly heighten the emotions viewers experience. They contribute significantly to the process through which viewers suspend disbelief and enter the fantasy world of the story. Media producers know that violence is an important technique in holding audience attention. This is why it is used with such frequency. People also are drawn to violent representations out of curiosity. Such representations offer a way to learn about experiences that most people will never encounter.

Cultures of Violence

What can explain the terrible collective acts of violence that human beings have wrought throughout history? How were the horrors of the Nazi holocaust allowed to occur? What motivates the hundreds of people committing suicide bombings? How has the US brought itself to use torture in the new millennium? Obviously these phenomena can't be explained away with drive theory or assertions of mass insanity. They are cultural matters deriving from the collective understandings groups or societies develop about when violent action is appropriate. Tradition provides the most easily understood rationale for violent action – the recognition that crimes and wars have taken place in the past and similar conflicts need to be dealt with in the present. Societies need police and armies to defend themselves and serving in these capacities is an honorable occupation. Of course, different cultures have addressed conflict in different ways. Historian Richard Slotkin has written about the way violence unified the colonies that became the United States. To Slotkin violence has always informed America's national identity, beginning with assaults by American settlers against the people they found on the new land, to the revolt of the American colonists against their European sponsors, to the American capture and importation of African people as slaves, to the annexation of Mexican territories, to the American Civil War.[15]

Societies legitimize violence by authorizing law enforcement and the military to commit violence on their behalf. Violence is justified in the name of justice and liberty. For this reason, societies generally sanction police or military justice only as a defensive measure. This is what made the US-led 2003 action against Iraq so controversial. When no weapons of mass destruction or terrorist connections were found, the defense argument lost its primary rationale and the legitimacy of the action was weakened. Some nations and people justify violence because of its efficiency. Individuals or groups with unmet needs become tempted by the prospect of getting what they want by using force to get it quickly. Robbery is faster and less exhausting than work; military attack is more expedient than diplomacy. Scapegoating happens when people are afraid, in need, or when a crisis occurs they can't understand. Confusion results. And strangers or newcomers often get blamed for the problems, and sometimes get attacked because of this. René Girard has described a process whereby third parties become stand-ins for adversaries that a group cannot identify or directly assault.[16] Deep within the human psyche, Girard believes, people identify adversaries who compete with them for things they both want. The competition foments violence acted out against an available substitute opponent. For example, a person comes home frustrated from work and kicks the dog or lashes out at a partner. Or a group facing rising unemployment decides to blame an immigrant population.

All of these cultural roads to violence point to one basic fact – that human beings become violent when faced with fear, trauma, or unmet needs. They turn to violence as a means of coping. The question for people concerned with media violence is what relationship representations of violence have with the real thing. Does media violence make the problem worse? Or does it, as some people have argued, reduce human proclivities for aggressive behavior? One of the biggest mistakes made in considering these questions is thinking that everyone responds to media violence in the same way. People are very different. Their varying identities in terms of gender, age, and cultural background (among many other factors) play important roles in how they respond to media.

Media violence isn't for everyone. Its biggest audience is adolescent boys. Young men are socialized to view violent media as an important part of gender identification. Although viewing can be a solitary experience, the consumption of violent media – especially sports – is often a group activity. And the experience doesn't stop when the movie or game ends. It is revisited in conversation and reenacted in play, especially in computer games where participants usually are obliged to shoot their opponents. In some instances the ability to tolerate violent imagery is regarded by peers as a measure of a young man's strength or maturity. Just as boys are urged to tolerate or enjoy scenes of terror, girls learn to exhibit appropriate levels of sensitivity or disapproval.[17]

What about children? It is commonly assumed that children are more attracted to violent imagery and more vulnerable to its harmful effects, especially when it comes to imitation. Bruno Bettelheim is largely responsible for a belief circulated in the 1970s that children had a "natural" attraction to violence. In his widely read *The Uses of Enchantment: The Meaning and Importance of Fairy Tales*,[18] Bettelheim asserted that frightening stories help kids to understand their innate aggressive tendencies and to eventually control them as adults. These beliefs persist today and provide rationalizations, not only for the continued exposure that children experience through traditional fairy tales like "Little Red Riding Hood" and "Hansel and Gretel," but also in the invariably violent narratives of Disney feature films like *Chronicles of Narnia* (2005) and *Pirates of the Caribbean: Dead Man's Chest* (2006) that feature violent death as primary plot ingredients. Writing of the widespread use of violence in children's media, Maria Tatar states that "Bettelheim's views have become the prevailing orthodoxy on fairy tales is symptomatic of our cultural willingness to embrace the view that 'delinquent and violent' tendencies are part of human nature and that children, in particular, must learn to manage this innate behavior."[19]

Yet nowhere in the literature or science of media violence has there been any documentation that children are naturally disposed to violence. Despite this paucity of evidence, children remain at the center of the media violence debate. In part this is because topics like "childhood," "children's welfare," and "the death of childhood" work so effectively in emotionalizing political arguments. The meanings of such terms can be quite variable, ranging from references to innocent children that need adult protection, to menacing children who take weapons to school, to the inner child, the childlike adult, and the adult-like child. In other words, childhood is not a natural or fixed category. It is a screen upon which adults project their social anxieties and desires. The figure of the child has been used historically to promote issues ranging from environmentalism ("children inherit the earth") to tax reform ("mortgaging our children's future"). David Buckingham writes about the "politics of substitution" that childhood enables:

In a climate of growing uncertainty, invoking fears about children provides a powerful means of commanding public attention and support: campaigns against homosexuality are redefined as campaigns against pedophiles; campaigns against pornography become campaigns against child pornography; campaigns against immorality and Satanism become campaigns against ritualistic child abuse. Those who have the temerity to doubt claims about the epidemic proportions of such phenomena can easily therefore be stigmatized as hostile to children.[20]

When all else fails in the media violence debate, proponents of surveillance and censorship haul out the image of the helpless and vulnerable child. While it is true that children don't have the same capabilities as adults, it can also be said that these projections at times discredit the intelligence of young people and contribute to a distorted infantilization. Close examination of children's responses to violent cartoons, for example, reveals that they more often respond to the excitement or excess of imagery in general, what Tatar terms "burlesque violence," than to the purposeful brutality of "retaliatory violence." When children write their own fairy tales, they tend to avoid this latter type of violence and write happy endings for all of the characters.[21] Like adults, children do revel in the arousal and excitement of aggressive representation in what Michael Zuckerman termed the "sensation seeking" motive.[22] Parents often worry about children overidentifying with perpetrators of television or movie violence. Surprisingly, there is very little data on this. What the research has shown is that most children don't imagine themselves committing violence, although roughly half empathize with victims of violence.[23] Even less plausible is the "forbidden fruit" theory that children's desire is increased if attempts are made to restrict access to a program. A variety of studies in the 1970s disproved this widely accepted theory. [24]

Researching the Effects of Media Violence

Groups seeking to influence public policy know the importance of "objective" research in making their claims. Psychologists and other social scientists have sought to correlate exposure to violent media with certain "effects" among viewers – such as aggression, desensitization, or fear. Often this involves laboratory research studies in which violent films or videos are shown to groups of children or adults, who subsequently answer questions about aggression. These findings are compared to those from a control group exposed to non-violent media. Some researchers observe the behavior of study subjects after viewing the media or they create situations where aggressive acts (hitting an inflatable doll, for example) may take place. Frequently in these experiments, viewers of violent media do indeed exhibit relatively small and short-term predilections for increased aggression. Laboratory experiments have led researchers to believe that media violence leads people to imitate what they see on the screen in their own lives. How does this work? According to psychologist Leonard Berkowitz, aggressive behavior occurs when viewers of violent media experience situations that remind them of something they've seen in a representation.[25] Another psychologist, Dolf Zillmann, asserts that violent media make viewers so excited that ordinary behaviors become amplified into violent ones.[26]

Other empirical research employs surveys or data analysis conducted outside the laboratory. The more nuanced of these seek to measure the effect of long-term exposure to media violence, rather than the cause-and-effect consequence of a single viewing. This move into what has been termed "cultivation" research is seen as a more naturalistic approach to the measurement of media effects. One of the originators of cultivation theory, George Gerbner, writes, "Television is a centralized system of storytelling. Its drama, commercials, news, and other programs bring a relatively coherent system of images and messages into every home. That system cultivates from infancy the predisposition and preferences that used to be acquired from other 'primary sources.'"[27] In this light, cultivation describes the "contributions television viewing makes to viewer conceptions of social reality."[28]

Generally speaking, there are two big problems in "scientifically" studying media violence. The first problem stems from how terribly difficult it is to study complex human behavior. A researcher first needs to figure out how to isolate the behavior and then to establish whether one thing or many things cause it. Human violence is influenced by many elements: brain chemistry, environment, upbringing, culture, and the immediate circumstances around it. Studying any one of these factors by itself is quite a challenge. Then add the complexity of the ways people consume, interpret, and are influenced by the media. People do not simply view a TV show or a deodorant advertisement and then robotically go out and act upon this experience. They enjoy, transform, reject, ignore, remember or forget the messages they receive. How do you study that?

The second problem has to do with logic. Most scientific studies set out to prove a correlation between watching violent media and a behavioral change. Perhaps a study shows that boys who see the *Doom* or *King Kong* (both 2005) movies are more likely to smash their toys. There is a correlation between watching the movies and doing the smashing. But this doesn't necessarily mean that the boys responded because of the movie. Perhaps a portion of the movie or an external element affected their behavior. Simple as this sounds, this problem of logic has dogged much of the science on media violence. Well-designed research studies can rule out some of the distorting effects of outside variables, but such studies are expensive and time-consuming. Major categories of empirical media violence research include laboratory research, field studies, and longitudinal (long-term) research.

Laboratory and Field Research

When most people think about the science of media violence they are thinking about laboratory research findings. This is the largest category of research and the one type of research capable of clearly proving cause-and-effect relationships. It is relatively quick and less expensive than extensive studies involving field research, interviews, or the long-term tracking of research subjects. For all of these reasons, empirical findings from laboratory experiments have been sought by groups seeking definitive answers about media violence. Laboratory experiments have been the centerpiece of what has been called the "effects" field in media violence.

Overall, the laboratory studies of the effects of media violence have shown small, short-term increases in aggressive behavior among participants viewing violent material. In one early and widely referenced study conducted in the 1960s by O. I. Lovaas, children in several cohorts were exposed to violent and non-violent cartoons.[29] In one of the cohorts the children who had seen the violent material exhibited a slightly more violent attitude immediately afterwards. In another group, viewers of both violent and non-violent films became more aggressive. Although the study was publicized later as "proving" the negative effects of media violence, the amount of influence the films had was relatively small and not long-acting. In another study conducted by C. W. Mueller and E. Donnerstein, subjects viewed aggressive, humorous, or neutral films and then were offered the chance to act aggressively.[30] Participants who had seen the aggressive or humorous films were more aggressive than those who had seen the neutral material. But in this instance no significant difference could be found between responses to the aggressive and the humorous films, leading observers to conclude that the aggressive behavior might have resulted from being excited or from "arousal," as one paper expressed it. These studies typify much of the laboratory research on media violence in that they can be said to have yielded evidence about the effects of viewing aggressive material. But they have been criticized for the overall weakness of their findings.

One of the most comprehensive assessments of media violence laboratory research was conducted in the late 1990s by psychologist Jonathan L. Freedman.[31] According to Freedman, many references by groups like the

American Medical Association and the American Academy of Psychiatry to large numbers of media violence studies – ranging from 1,000 to 3,500 in some accounts – can be sourced to a single frequently cited statement in a National Institute of Mental Health report of the 1980s that there existed approximately 2,500 *publications* on the topic. This is hardly the same as a comparable number of empirical studies. Freedman suggests that the question of the number of studies may really be an issue of semantics. After exhaustive investigation, Freedman found that the media violence "effects" literature actually consisted of 200 pieces of non-duplicated research of varying degrees of scientific legitimacy. The most credible of these studies were able to document but minimal correlations or trace "effects" resulting in increased aggressive behavior among those studied.

Most often the effects of media violence were demonstrated through laboratory experiments, which in more recent years have been criticized for the way they decontextualize media in environments quite unlike everyday viewing. Of the 87 laboratory experiments Freedman examined, he asserts that 37 percent supported the effects hypothesis, 41 percent disproved it, and 22 percent were inconclusive. This means that in the aggregate the research says that media violence *does not correlate* to aggression. Studies using survey techniques produced similar ambiguities, showing an aggregate positive correlation between violent media and aggression between 0.1 and 0.2. This means that the studies were able to show that but 1–4 percent of the aggression expressed by the people surveyed could be attributed to media violence. Statisticians would consider this an extremely weak correlation. These findings were compromised further in their use of smaller samples. Also, many failed when attempts were made to reproduce the findings in a second study.[32]

Finally, there are several other problems with laboratory research. The most commonly heard is that the laboratory experimentation takes place in an environment dramatically different from one where the effects of media violence might be diluted by distraction, conversation, or outside influence. Also, laboratory research is more vulnerable to what has been termed "experimenter demand," that is, the thinking by research subjects that they are expected to exhibit some kind of behavior because of the experiment. Put another way, the artificiality of the laboratory environment makes people behave differently than they would normally.

Field experiments constitute another broad category of effects, generally favored because they provide a more natural environment than the laboratory. They also tend to be more long-term. As discussed in the introduction to this book, one of the most famous field studies was carried out in 1971 by Feshbach and Singer, who studied 625 boys in seven residential boarding academies and reform schools in California and New York.[33] In both types of institution the boys' access to television was controlled for six weeks, with half being permitted to watch only non-violent programs and the other violent shows. Astonishingly, the boys in the violent program cohort exhibited fewer acts of violent behavior – like acting up in class, fighting, or breaking things – than the non-violent cohort. It turned out that the non-violent cohort were made unhappy because they couldn't watch their favorite violent shows. While many other field experiments have shown a relationship between viewing violence and aggressive behavior, the Feshbach and Singer study holds significance in pointing out one of the major drawbacks of field research. Studying groups in natural environments over long periods of time limits the researchers' ability to correct for extraneous factors that might muddle their findings. In this case researchers didn't take into account the effect of the boys' existing viewing preferences – and that those preferences might override or cause a backfire in how the boys reacted to the study protocol.

Long-Term Research

The most famous study of the long-term effects of media violence was conducted from 1960 to 1982 by psychologists Leonard D. Eron and L. Rowell Huesmann.[34] The idea behind what came to be called the "22-Year Study" was to look at the difference between children who grew up with violent media and those who were not exposed to such material. Over the years the findings reported that aggression grew among boys, but not among girls, who watched violent shows. Eron and Huesmann reported their findings to the Office of the US Surgeon General in the 1970s and to the National Institute of Mental Health. Their findings were cited by Congress in the 1996 Telecommunications Act that put in place the V-chip requirement in later years, stating that "Studies have shown that children exposed to violent video programming at a young age have a higher tendency for violent and aggressive behavior later in life than children not so exposed."[35]

In 2000, Pulitzer Prize-winning journalist Richard Rhodes took up the media violence issue in a report entitled "The Media Violence Myth."[36] In preparing the report, Rhodes interviewed major figures in the media violence field like Eron and Huesmann, pressing them to answer critics who had questioned the validity of their findings. Eron told Rhodes of the pressures that had been put upon researchers by government officials' who wanted them to find negative effects – stating that the scientists really hadn't concluded that their research proved much of a link between viewing habits and later aggression. Only a few boys seemed to have changed their habits over the years and most weren't affected at all. Heusmann later admitted that the "proof" in the study that had fueled so much fervor and resulted in legislative action was derived from a handful of boys and that he and his collaborators had never thought that media alone could be the cause of antisocial behavior. Huesmann has "deliberately misrepresented his findings," Rhodes charges. Huesmann has claimed that there is a strong relationship between "early violence viewing and later criminality." Yet his conclusion was based on only three cases among 145 adult males who watched action television shows as children.

"There's no evidence that mock violence makes people violent, and there's some evidence that it makes them more peaceful," Rhodes concludes.[37] Rhodes is also critical of the work of Brandon Centerwall, another scientist whose studies are frequently cited by legislators and other advocates of restricting media violence.[38] Centerwall, a psychiatrist whose research was a mainstay of the Senate Judiciary Committee's 1999 report, "Children, Violence and the Media: A Report for Parents and Policy Makers," claims that the introduction of television doubles the violent crime rate. Rhodes cites evidence showing that violent crime rates in Europe and Japan either stayed the same or declined in the years following the introduction of television. Rhodes argues that Centerwall's theory is also contradicted by falling US crimes rates despite continuing and even increased exposure to media.

Content Analysis

Science also has been applied to media violence through content analysis. In 1998 the National Television Violence Study (NTVS) determined that 60 percent of broadcast programming contained some form of violence.[39] Conducted by a consortium of major research universities, the NTVS was the largest effort to analyze television programming to date, employing 300 people to quantify occurrences of violence in 10,000 hours of TV from a variety of broadcast and cable sources. Called into being by Congress, the study noted that "television violence" was a huge, complex, and often ill-defined topic. Along with efforts to categorize the various forms and contexts of television violence, the study identified three broad and widely accepted "risks" of viewing violent media: "learning aggressive attitudes and behaviors, desensitization to violence, and increased fear of becoming victimized by violence."[40]

Like reports and statements issued by the AMA, APA, and AACAP, the NTVS established itself on a foundation of preexisting research. Asserting a clear causal link between media violence and its reenactment in society, the NTVS stated that "hundreds of studies have proven the link between violence and aggressive behavior."[41] Close examination of the NTVS reports and the statements from the professional organizations reveals that none of them conducted original research on the "causal hypothesis," as it has been termed. They simply assumed that it must be true and began work based on that belief. To NTVS researchers, the logic that television influences behavior is simple and clear: "A multi-billion dollar advertising industry is built on the premise."[42]

Despite its unexamined acceptance of the causal hypothesis, the NTVS made a major contribution to the discourse of media violence in its explication of the many varieties of TV violence, its emphasis on the context in which the violence occurs, and its restraint in articulating the social impact of media violence. Contradicting conventional wisdom, the NTVS stated that

> Violence on television need not lead to the reinforcement of aggressive attitudes and behaviors. If the consequences of violence are demonstrated, if violence is shown to be regretted or punished, if its perpetrators are not glamorized, if the act of violence is not seen as justified, if in general violence is shown in a negative light, then the portrayal of violence may not create negative consequences.[43]

From this seemingly sensible commentary in a major national study one might get the impression that the media violence field was moving toward some kind of consensus. Not so. The problem is that many scholars who study media just don't buy the effects argument, no matter how carefully it is articulated. Consider this statement on the first page of *Ill Effects: The Media/Violence Debate*, a book one might expect to offer a balanced account of the debate.[44] "The claims about the possible 'effects of violent media' are not just false, they range from the daft to the mischievous,"[45] write Martin Barker and Julian Petley, adding that questions about media violence have "the same status as those who, for centuries, insistently asked if human illnesses, the death of pigs, thunderstorms, and crop failures were the result of witchcraft."[46] Like many other works by media scholars, *Ill Effects* condemns the flaws of empirical effects research while reveling in the presumed benefits and "pleasures" that come from such material.

Then there is the entertainment industry, which has claimed that the effects claims are overstated and politically motivated. In his 1968 testimony before the congressional "National Commission on the Causes and Prevention of Violence," Jack Valenti, president of the Motion Picture Association of America (MPAA), stated that violence is an inevitable and necessary part of movie making: "Throughout the whole history of drama, violence is a common ingredient. That goes without saying. The very nature of drama is conflict."[47] The media conglomerates assert that they are simply providing what audiences want to see. If demand were lacking, programming would change. Of course, the argument that content is audience-driven is the exact opposite of the effects view that content controls audience thinking. Both are but fragmentary elements of a communicative process that not only encompasses both types of exchange, but also is affected by narrative genre, program format, and type of audience, production technologies, and delivery mechanisms, among other factors.

Finally, a correlation is not the same as a cause. It is simply an association. The correlation of media violence to aggression could just as easily mean that aggressive people prefer violent media. Many of the young men involved in the past two decades of school shootings have shared characteristics beyond a diet of violent media. Aggression is a highly complex phenomenon, whose etiology includes a wide variety of psychological, social, and circumstantial factors. "Measuring" aggression in relationship to such an equally complex substance as the media is incredibly difficult. Many argue that it is an impossible task. At best empirical science can provide but a small part of our understanding of media violence.

The War of the Professors

Part of the problem in getting agreement on the media violence question comes from the cycle of hysteria discussed earlier that starts with reasonable concern but results in a frenzied public shouting match. Worried parents and child advocates, politicians hungry for votes, and ratings-driven news media all put pressure on the world of academic "experts" to provide them with ammunition against media violence. From the other side, the entertainment industry, libertarians, and free speech advocates demand justifications for more violent media. But the world of scholarly research is really just another marketplace, with many vendors desperate to sell a product to get themselves book deals, grants, or simply tenure. This pressure encourages researchers to make dramatic claims for their work and sometimes to exaggerate the significance of findings.

The anti-media violence side has gotten most of the attention until recently. After all, who can blame parents for being worried that their kids will become influenced by the growing barrage of movies, TV shows, and games using ever more spectacular displays of human carnage to sell themselves? Family-oriented foundations, legislators, religious organizations, mental health professionals, and the law-enforcement community have all sought answers based on the common-sense logic that all violence in the media must have some connection to human aggression. They've largely gone to the scientific community for answers with the expectation that behavioral psychologists might be able to prove the negative "effects" of media. Respected members of the social science professions, many of whom have spent their careers studying other similar community health issues with behavioral components – like addiction and crime – have an entire field devoted to providing quantitative data about media violence. However, the findings have been mixed and have not shown that media violence by itself is a major cause of crime or aggression. Unfortunately, the research has sometimes been interpreted by non-scientists more interested in finding a scapegoat for a social problem than in bringing forward a more nuanced discussion of the issue. That's the kind of sensationalized fear-mongering that makes headlines, gets people on talk shows, and satisfies voters. But it takes a toll. The shrill rhetoric of the anti-media violence crowd alienates moderate observers and drowns out other perspectives, including those that might help the problem by looking beyond a futile "just-say-no" posture that will never convince curious kids that the stuff is bad for them. The just-say-no approach also upsets producers and free-speech advocates who see it as a suggestion of censorship.

The pro-media violence side (for lack of a better term) has been somewhat sheepish because of the obvious self-interest of the entertainment industry in justifying its enormously profitable market in selling violent material. This is why the manufacturers of violent media historically have sought to put the onus on retailers and consumers by promoting labeling systems that let them off the hook. Owing to their large role in the American economy, entertainment producers have largely gotten their way and been permitted to make as much violent material as they can sell, although they also use this argument to justify sexual content. Efforts by anti-media violence groups have been thwarted in part by arguments from economic conservatives who say that the marketplace is the final arbiter of what the people want. Opposition has risen and political pressure has grown from liberals as well, especially among civil liberties groups that have entered the fray to defend the free-speech rights of producers. On the academic side, intellectuals in the humanities first argued that violent mass entertainment was encouraging people to indulge their most primitive aggressive instincts. Extremists argued that the commercial media system was a mechanism to convince people to buy products. After all, the advertising industry was based on just this premise. Later academics conducting audience studies and media research found that people were much more independent in their thinking and were usually not influenced by media violence very much at all. These scholars asserted that people could be quite critical in viewing media and tended to take ideas from what they watched that could improve their lives and help them to be more satisfied.

So the dissenting camps in the media violence debate both disagreed about the effects of media violence and approached the problem from very different angles. The anti-media violence side made up of parents, teachers, and psychologists that had to deal with the day-to-day difficulties of unruly children and twisted teenagers thought that violent media producers and academics who liked to discuss how violent movies worked and why people liked them didn't really care about the way violent fare might do damage. The pro-media violence group of media professionals, free-speech advocates, and film studies professors thought that their opponents were exaggerating the negative effects of media and blaming media for a host of problems that really had other causes. This produced a weird standoff. The anti-media violence side ended up having its say, with congress voting in the V-chip legislation and attempting to set limits on games and internet speech. The producers knuckled down with voluntary labeling that pretended to protect people. Everyone seemed to have gotten something from the battle. But nothing really changed.

The battle got a little hotter and more public around 2000, with a flurry of publications: David Buckingham's *After the Death of Childhood: Growing Up in the Age of Electronic Media*, David Gauntlett and Annette Hill's *TV Living: Television, Culture, and Everyday Life*, Jib Fowles's *The Case for Media Violence*, Richard Rhodes's essay "The Media Violence Myth," and Jonathan Freedman's book *Media Violence and Aggression: Assessing the Scientific Evidence*.[48] There had been a few prior books taking issue with the anti-media violence argument, but most of them had been dismissed by the mainstream media violence community as academic gibberish or ploys to pander to the entertainment industry. The new publications by credible scholars emerged in the context of other writing gaining wider attention from media and cultural studies academics like Henry Giroux, Barry Glassner, Jeffrey Goldstein, Henry Jenkins, Mike Males, and Vivian Sobchack, who had been bringing media fear-mongering and scapegoating out into the open.[49]

This work, in turn, was built upon the broader interdisciplinary movements that had brought into question narrow academic traditions in anthropology, education, and sociology that had measured human cultures throughout history according to the standards of Western civilization and patriarchal authority. In anthropology, younger scholars from diverse perspectives challenged the colonial agenda of European and American scholars who viewed "other" cultures as primitive and inferior. In education, liberal reformers questioned the hierarchies that said knowledge was always passed down from teachers to students. In sociology, reformers took issue with standardized definitions of what counted as "normal."

The spate of books that appeared in 2000 expressed a growing academic consensus that sought to restore balance in a conversation about media violence that had been dominated by reactionary rhetoric, flawed research, and distorted accounts of legitimate scientific studies. Buckingham exposed ways parents' and children's groups had been deceived about the threats of violent media, Gauntlett and Fowles took apart anti-media violence arguments by pointing out logical flaws and bias, Rhodes tracked down leading scientific figures in the media violence debate and documented ways their findings had been exaggerated or misstated. Freedman researched the empirical evidence and revealed that most of the science had failed to prove the case against media violence. Soon scores of respected humanities professors and intellectuals were lining up with letters and petitions to groups like the AMA and the ACAP, imploring them to back down on blanket condemnations of violent movies and games.

Then came 9/11. That morning witnessed the most spectacular display of media violence in the history of human communication. In many ways, it reset the register on which violence would be recorded and understood forever after. But in other ways, media coverage of 9/11 simply replicated ways of seeing of violence that were very familiar to most people. It was different because the spectacular disaster really did happen, but also strangely familiar because the news footage could be recognized to be "just like a movie." The years following have been a time of *détente* in the media violence war. For a while following 9/11 it didn't seem relevant to talk about violent TV shows or toys in the wake of such a huge national trauma. The entertainment industry even delayed the launch of certain movies like *Collateral Damage* (2002) and games that might seem insensitive as the nation waited, worried, and mourned. But before very long the national obsession with terrorism became just too much to resist. TV shows like *Alias*, *24*, and *Sleeper Cell* began to appear that featured espionage, terror attacks, and even the torture of enemy combatants. Production of apocalypse and school shooting movies picked up with works like Gus Van Sant's *Elephant* (2003). By 2003 the nation's most popular computer game was *Counterstrike*, in which players could choose sides in a Middle Eastern combat zone. Public concern over media violence escalated in 2005 as incidents of teenage violence and lawsuits appeared over two computer games that dominated the market that year: the Sony PlayStation format *Grand Theft Auto: San Andreas* and its main Microsoft X-Box competitor *Halo 2*. Then came *Splinter Cell: Chaos Theory* (2005), pitting agents from China, Japan, Korea, and the United States against each other. Meanwhile, new strains of violent television and movies continue to emerge. The film, media, and cultural studies communities have continued to assess these evolving forms, but mostly under the radar of public view.

Film and Media Studies

Nothing could be further from the scientific media violence "effects" field than the new interdisciplinary subjects of film, media, and cultural studies. But before these fields emerged in the 1970s and 1980s, by far the largest group of intellectuals to think about media violence were professors of English, who always comprised a large segment of university faculties. In fulfilling needs for basic writing instruction, English departments brought to higher education hundreds of thousands of PhDs who had written dissertations examining stories of heroism, love, ambition, conflict, crime, and war. In a related development, film studies emerged in the 1960s, largely within English departments, using movies to teach writing and critical analysis. Often the interest in discussing film led to the establishment of informal cinema societies on campuses, which would later blossom into film programs and departments. Similar use of television and movies in the social sciences would lead to the development of communication studies programs, which focused more on the mechanics of media. In many instances these disciplines of the moving image would converge or overlap, especially as they addressed production. The point is that for four decades a robust scholarly apparatus has existed for the interpretation and analysis of movies, television, and related media – with an extensive theoretical literature addressing how visual media work and how audiences receive them.

Discussion in mainstream media about movies and television programs is generally limited to a simple description of the idea behind the show linked to brief mentions on newscasts or to promotional appearances of celebrities on talk shows. Movie reviews often are little more than an expanded version of this descriptive material, and are carried by newspapers and network news programs primarily as information or promotion. In their infancy, the disciplines of film and media studies married this informational approach to movies with the traditional tools of literary study used in the field of English. Early film studies focused on how movies used plot, theme, character development, and filmic technique to move viewers through stories, build their expectations, and deliver satisfying conclusions. Many of today's print and television reviewers of movies still discuss films in these terms. As the study of film became more serious, the discussion began to include the role that actors and directors played, often looking at their individual expressive styles in what was termed "auteur" criticism.

This paralleled the recognition that movies could be grouped into stylistic genres – like drama, comedy, and action – that operated with their own sets of rules and formulas. For example, comedies from the silent era onward developed specific conventions for the use of violence to heighten humorous effects and to keep audiences excited. Borrowing techniques from vaudeville, early movie comedies were full of fighting, calamity, and destruction to make their stories more exciting and "funny." Special effects technologies emerged to create violent spectacles that audiences of early movies came to expect. The comedic styles of Charlie Chaplin, Harold Lloyd, and Buster Keaton featured simple falls, collisions, accidents, and other mishaps that viewers could easily understand and follow. Similar principles of physical visual humor are with us today in teen movies from *Animal House* (1978) to *My Super Ex-Girlfriend* (2006) and in family comedies such as *The Shaggy Dog* (2006) and *Monster House* (2006).

Crime is another huge genre driven by violence. Even before the invention of moving pictures, people bought dime novels and cheaply printed stories of cops and robbers. Viewers got a vicarious thrill from watching the stories unfold and seeing the spectacle of police tracking down criminals. Early in the twentieth century public concern emerged over the harm that might result from crime stories. Was such voyeurism good for people? Would children imitate police or see criminals as heroes? As movies grew to be a mass entertainment medium in the 1920s and 1930s, films about crime and gangsters became enormously popular, magnifying in fictional form the real crime and mob activity in the Roaring Twenties and the Prohibition years. Anticipating a crackdown on the movie industry, the MPPDA in 1927 engaged leading authorities in the fields of criminology, psychology, and psychiatry to prepare a report on the effects of gangster movies on viewers. In a paper entitled "Crime and the Motion Picture" distributed that year, psychiatrist Carleton Simon stated:

> I do not believe that any legitimate melodrama of crime, any detective story or any motion picture dealing with the life of underworld characters, has ever been the sole incentive to or motivation of criminal behavior . . . the

great mass of medical and psychological observation is set against the possibility that the witnessing of a motion picture could be an effective stimulus to behavior previously inconsistent with the individual's standard of conduct.[50]

The gangster movies of the 1930s did not occur in a social vacuum. Many critics attributed their popularity to their function as morality tales about the consequences of wanting money and possessions so much that one turns to crime, becomes a gangster, and ultimately is brought to justice by violent means. It's telling in this regard that the MPPDA Production Code put in place during this era to regulate the content of movies dictated that criminal activity "shall never be presented in such a way as to throw sympathy with crime as against law and justice or to inspire others with a desire for imitation." [51]

These principles created the template for movie and television crime dramas for the decades that followed. They help explain why the public appetite for violence always has seemed so natural and why screen violence has remained so satisfying. Crime movies frequently are little more than classic tales of good against evil with heroes and their opponents pitted in eternal conflicts with inevitable outcomes. Some theorists believe that such stories provide comfort and become popular in the US when the nation is experiencing a time of distress, such as during the Depression years when gangster films flourished. Sometimes the roles of good guys and bad guys have become reversed, as in *Bonnie and Clyde* (1967), a film that appeared at the height of the Vietnam War and featured a romantic criminal couple with whom many viewers identified. With the elimination of the Production Code in the 1960s, Hollywood became more willing to take risks with films that glamorized violent criminality. Examples range from series like *The Godfather* (1972, 1974, 1990) and *Rambo* (1982, 1985, 1988) movies to more recent films like *Oceans 12* (2004), *The Black Dahlia* (2006), and *Déjà Vu* (2006). Men play tough guys in most of these movies, with the notable exception of a few films like *Thelma and Louise* (1991) and *Guncrazy* (1992).

Crime dramas remain enormously popular in movies, television, and computer games. TV series featuring individual detectives like *Kojak, Columbo, Baretta, Magnum P.I., Mannix,* and more recently *Monk,* play out morality tales as audiences identify with the familiar personality of the lead sleuth. Ensemble shows like *Law and Order, Homicide, Cold Case, The Shield,* and *CSI* add the dimension of multiple narratives that bring greater complexity. When the good-guy police or detectives use violence against criminals, audiences experience a degree of satisfaction because the violence is deemed necessary and justified. This reinforces the broader social endorsement of aggression by those it sanctions to commit violence on its behalf. A similar attitude provides enjoyment to viewers of war movies in which violence is committed on a greater scale. Crime and war programs have received criticism when perpetrators or enemies are consistently cast as people of specific social classes, races, or nationalities. At times this has been done intentionally, as during World War II when Japanese and German "enemies" were portrayed with negative stereotypes. In more recent years, reality television shows like *Cops* frequently feature working-class, African American, or Latino people in footage of "live" chases or arrests. Police dramas also have received criticism for the way they present crime out of context, with little consideration of the reasons why people break the law or the long-term consequences of their actions to them and their victims.

The classic conflicts in violent dramas became even more cartoonish in the genre of the American western movie that also made its first appearance in the early days of motion pictures. Westerns are distinctive as a category in two primary areas: the ways they depict the American frontier and their treatment of masculine identity. Westerns appeared when movies first were gaining mass appeal with films like *Hell's Hinges* (1916) and *Straight Shooting* (1917). Like gangster movies, the western came into full bloom in the 1920s and 1930s with films like *The Gold Rush* (1925) and *The Virginian* (1929), *Way Out West* (1938), and *Stagecoach* (1939), followed by classics like *High Noon* (1952), *The Searchers* (1956), and *Rio Bravo* (1959).

Such films depicted the American frontier as a colonial wilderness of utopian promise and anarchistic lawlessness, populated by primitive natives, pioneering settlers, and lethal criminals. The land needed taming by maverick lawmen, gun-toting civilians, or the military, for whom women served as dutiful (and often victimized) wives or prostitutes. Racism and sexism remained central to the western movie genre in later decades as well as to the many television series from *The Lone Ranger*, *The Rifleman*, and *Bonanza* through later series like *The Wild Wild West*, *Little House on the Prairie*, and the HBO series *Deadwood*.

Masculine identity focused sharply on the image of the violent and emotionally detached individual operating within a rigidly defined moral order to be defended often without external support in the barren new land. White-skinned good guys battled white-skinned bad guys, who both found themselves frequently in conflict with indigenous peoples or Mexicans. Like gangster movies, the plots of most westerns were driven by a near fanatical materialism and struggle for gold, money, land, and sometimes women as trophies for the winning side. Some critics have commented upon the exceptional treatment given to men's bodies in western movies and TV shows in which extended scenes of fist fights, beatings, bloody gun battles, bodily mutilation, and torture accounted for much of the screen time.[52] Further discussion of the implications of such bodily punishment for the identities of boys and men will be taken up in the next chapter. Without doubt westerns played a powerful role in establishing the image of a "real man" in American society as a tough and aggressive individual ready to fight and willing to kill if provoked or threatened.

With the suspension of the Production Code in 1968, Sam Peckinpah directed the hyperviolent *The Wild Bunch* (1969) that rewrote the way gunfights were shot and edited by introducing over a dozen cameras filming a single action scene and a rapid editing style that increased the number of cuts from the average 600 for a feature to over 3,500. More notable still was Peckinpah's claim that the incredible blood, gore, and death in *The Wild Bunch* was intended to shock audiences into despair over the "real" human atrocities of Vietnam news footage to which audiences had become desensitized by daily viewing. The idea that violence on the screen might move viewers to pacifism has a history that parallels the development of photography as a recording medium. It inspired generations of photojournalists and filmmakers to record the horrors of war and present fictionalized atrocities. Little has been written about whether or not these efforts were successful. Taking a somewhat different approach in their critiques of violence have been revisionist westerns like *Little Big Man* (1970), *Dances With Wolves* (1970), and *The Unforgiven* (1972). These movies have pointed out the injustices that went unquestioned or unnoticed in mythic images of the American West.

Science fiction movies are sometimes compared to westerns in the way they place their stories in a lawless and untamed wilderness. Of course they generally do this in the context of a futuristic fantasy or an imaginary technology. Turn-of-the-century French filmmaker Georges Méliès created one of the first sci-fi films with his 1902 *Journey to the Moon*. The first science fiction features – movies like *Metropolis* (1927) and *Woman in the Moon* (1929) appeared in the 1920s after World War I and are said to express society's anxieties about the horrible potentials of technology. Science fiction horror films began appearing after World War II, expressing similar social anxieties about atomic weapons and global destruction. Many scholars say that movies in the 1950s, like *The Thing from Another World* and *When Worlds Collide* (both 1951), about creatures from outer space and aliens who looked like people were really stories about America's foreign enemies and the fear of communist infiltration. Because science fiction movies were often cast in future societies and different worlds, they frequently were seen as metaphoric critiques of real-life social conditions.

The Pleasure of Terror

Social scientists conducting media violence research can be uninformed about perspectives from media studies – and they consequently approach media violence with a disciplinary bias. Social science "effects" researchers often apply what might be termed a "correspondence" or "transmission" theory of communication that sees information moving unilaterally and unproblematically from image to viewer. People who study media know this is incorrect. Informed by theories of language and reception, media studies recognizes that a movie can convey many kinds of messages simultaneously that will be understood differently by different viewers. How one perceives a piece of media is affected by the knowledge, experience, and background one brings to the encounter, as well as the viewing context. Moreover, audiences do not simply take in what they are shown. Instead they engage in an ongoing exchange with the movie in which they develop expectations about what will happen next. In the process viewers may accept, reject, or ignore parts of the message – or they may invent meanings quite different than those intended by the maker. Meaning is always a matter of negotiation. This is why efforts to pin down correlations between media violence and aggression have been so difficult.

Also, media violence is extremely difficult to define and quantify. Is it simply a matter of depicting physical harm? Does it need to be aggressive or intentional? What about accidents or natural disasters? Does psychological torment count? What about verbal or implied violence? Are there degrees of violence? Is justified violence better for viewers than the gratuitous variety? What about humorous violence? Sports? The answer is that no one really knows. As James Potter wrote in his landmark overview of the effects field, *On Media Violence*, "In the literature on media violence, definitions of violence vary widely. There is no consensus. . . . These conditions make it very difficult to synthesize findings across studies."[53] The NTVS grappled with this problem in asserting differential effects from different forms of media violence. Potter was one of the senior investigators of the NTVS, which stated in its summary report:

> The same research that shows that televised violence can have harmful effects also demonstrates that not all violence portrayals are problematic. There are many ways to depict violence. For example, the violence may occur on-

screen and be shown graphically, or it may occur off-screen but be clearly implied. Violent acts may be shown close-up or at a distance. There are also differences in the types of characters who commit violence and their reasons for doing so. And there are differences in the outcomes of violence – some depictions focus on the pain and suffering of victims, whereas others avoid showing the negative consequences of physical aggression. Simply put, not all portrayals of violence are the same. Their context can vary in many important ways. Studies show that the way in which violence is presented helps to determine whether portrayal might be harmful to viewers.[54]

Beyond the issue of whether or not media violence causes harm is the more provocative question of why people choose to watch. What desires does media violence satisfy? What pleasures, if any, does it provide? How does media violence work?

Part of the answer is media-specific. Movies, television, computer games, and print media structure information differently. In a movie theater viewers are more easily drawn into the viewing space of the screen that enables the suspension of disbelief in the artifice of the film. Distraction is minimized spatially by a darkened theater and temporally by the absence of commercial interruptions, as well as the social convention of remaining seated throughout the movie. In contrast, television must fight for attention, functioning as a source of entertainment, news, and background noise. Rather than delivering discrete narratives, network television offers a jumble of program segments, commercials, and new updates that viewers experience in what Raymond Williams termed a "flow."[55] Satellite, cable, and recording technologies enable programs to be manipulated, repeated, and rescheduled. Computer games and the internet introduce the element of interactivity.

The assertion is often made that violence in the media is becoming increasingly graphic and "real." In fact the opposite is taking place. Part of what makes media violence appealing to viewers is the extent to which it is anesthetized and transformed by production technologies. Director Sam Peckinpah is regarded as one of the pioneers in such work, beginning with his film *The Wild Bunch*. In that film gunfights were depicted using shots from numerous cameras to create a sense of spatial movement and depth. Rapidly changing footage displayed at normal speed was intercut with slow-motion imagery that drew in viewers at key moments. More recently, Steven Spielberg's *Saving Private Ryan* (1998) – a film that many war veterans say captured the genuine "feel" of battle – relied on a veritable smorgasbord of techniques and tricks to generate the sensation of verisimilitude. Manipulations of camera shutter speeds created a jerky "pixilated" experience of action scenes, as did the intentional interference with camera sync.

Use of an "image shaker" gave the impression of nearby explosions. Exaggerations of handheld camera movements – typically corrected by flexicam technology – gave some scenes the "realistic" sense of documentary footage shot on the run. Tampering with the coating of lenses gave some scenes an eerie atmospheric look. Chemical treatments to the film increased the contrast and density of shadows. As Stephen Prince observed, "These techniques gave the violence an elaborate and explicit aesthetic frame, which was intensified by the picture's narrative of heroism and moral redemption. The violence was not raw, that is, it was not real. It was staged for the camera and filtered through various effects and technologies."[56]

This aestheticization of violence makes it tolerable and enjoyable. Through the pyrotechnics of cinematic technology and special effects, portrayals of such "cartoon violence" become bombastic spectacles of excess. The entertainment industry is well aware of how this process works. As the technology of computer-generated special effects has improved in the past decade, its costs have fallen dramatically. This is another reason for the proliferation of violent spectacles. Besides appealing to the broadest domestic audience demographics and besides their international marketability in non-English-speaking "after-markets," movies heavy with digital special effects are cheap to make. This financial incentive not only drives the selection of films a production company will make, it increasingly is a factor in how movies initially are conceived. Movie violence has become the central idea upon which many films are based.

The "New Violence"

More than one critic has commented that violence has become such a driving force in many action films that spectacular moments like long car chases, nuclear bomb explosions, earthquakes, and photon beam blasts have achieved more prominence than character, plot, or storyline. In fact, one of the funnier aspects of studying contemporary action films is that the occurrence of extraordinary pyrotechnics often makes no sense whatsoever. This is certainly true in such action thrillers as the *Crank* (2006), *Miami Vice* (2006), and *The Fast and the Furious: Tokyo Drift* (2006). The nonsensical character of movie violence has become so extreme that it has inspired a new subgenre of films – termed the "new violence" movies – that mimic or poke fun at action movies. Oliver Stone's *Natural Born Killers* (1994), Quentin Tarantino's *Kill Bill 1* (2003), *and Kill Bill 2* (2004), and *Grind House* (2006) all use violence to such excess that they make critical comments on the genre. New-violence films have also been produced by the growing movie industries in Japan, India, and other Asian nations. The hit Japanese cult movies *Battle Royale* (2000), *The Suicide Club* (2000), *Ichi the Killer* (2002), and *The Grudge* (2004) all use excessive violence with a sense of critique and have been rewarded at prestigious film festivals for the intelligent ways they examine violence in relationship to other social issues. The one problem with such postmodern copying or appropriation of older styles of violence is that audiences often don't grasp the irony or the joke. Many viewers walked out of films like *Natural Born Killers* and *Kill Bill* with the conviction that movie making has reached an all-time low and that impressionable viewers will probably imitate the violence the films depict. Indeed, many viewers are drawn to these new-violence movies exactly for the excitement that they derive from taking in the cartoonish violence the films provide. What is the real downside of the new-violence movies, if any? The answer is that few viewers will be moved to emulate the killers they see on the screen, but they may take away from the movies something even more problematic: an enhanced belief that the world is a violent place, that violence is a good way to solve problems, and that violent characters are people to be admired and emulated.

3

We are Afraid:
Media Violence and Society

Media violence may not provoke people to become aggressive or commit crimes, but it does something more damaging. Media violence convinces people that they live in a violent world and that violence is required to make the world safer. The anxieties and attitudes that result from these beliefs about the world have profound consequences in the way people live their lives and they way society is organized. People's behavior at home and in public, at work, at school, and in leisure activities becomes affected. Anxieties about violence influence the television people watch, what they read, and what they discuss with friends. They cast a shadow on the ways they plan their time, where they decide to go, and what they buy. Ultimately media violence takes a toll on the way people imagine their lives and how they think about the future. This anxious worldview is the result of a culture of violence that forges our core identities in fear.

Identity and Fear

From the minute you wake up in the morning you are told to be afraid. You are enveloped by the culture of fear. Get out of bed and go into the bathroom. Every product has a warning label: to swallow too much mouthwash will have a fatal consequence. Starting to make breakfast brings the awareness that many foods cause weight gain, contribute to illness, or contain harmful ingredients. Going out of the door you hear that the economy is slowing down, interest rates are rising, and that the terror alert level has been raised. Leaving the house you set the security code, walk to your car, and turn off the alarm. Getting in the car you look in a mirror and realize that you are alone. And you're afraid.

We live our daily lives enveloped in a culture of fear. Not simply a fear of immediate danger, but also a broader fear that we're doing something wrong or that we aren't all that we should be or could be. These feelings are no accident. They are not in any way a "natural" part of us. We get them from somewhere. They come from our friends, our family, and the media. Ironically, we get them from some of the people and things we really like. That's why they work. On a conscious level, we are aware that our immediate surroundings, the things we consume, and the broader world we inhabit are all fraught with dangers. We can minimize these dangers by knowing where they lurk, being smart about how we live, and protecting ourselves and our loved ones in every way we can. But safety comes with a price. To feel secure we alter the way we act, make compromises in what we want to achieve, and pay – on many levels – for a perception of safety. We do whatever is necessary to protect our health, we buy whatever products or services will help us look good and successfully integrate into society, and we support a legal system and legislature that will act on our behalf to protect us, using violent means – and even killing other people – if necessary. This is the true damage effected by media violence. The true "effects" of media violence create what veteran media scholar George Gerbner has called the "mean world" syndrome – the belief that our world is a dangerous place where simplistically defined forces of good and evil are continually in conflict, where movie-style heroes and villains really exist, and where violent force is necessary to sustain our ongoing well-being.[1]

This makes fear a part of who we are. It's more than an occasional scare from a horror movie or a phobia about germs or an airplane flight or Al Qaeda. Anxiety takes over our sense of who we are and who we might become. People experience so many fears in so many aspects of life that a feeling of fear starts to control them and their society. Much of news and entertainment is driven by stories that produce fear, and many of the consumer products we buy and use function to ward off various insecurities and anxieties.

Where does such thinking come from? Why does such anxiety persist in the absence of verifying evidence or logical inquiry? The answer is that collective fear is a social construction driven by money and sustained by social anxiety in an era of growing uncertainty. In recent years a number of well-researched books have discussed our skittish culture. Barry Glassner's *The Culture of Fear: Why Americans are Afraid of the Wrong Things*, largely criticizes hyperbolic news and entertainment media for frightening people.[2] David L. Altheide's *Creating Fear: News and the Construction of Crisis* discusses what he terms "the problem frame" that "promotes a discourse of fear that may be defined as the pervasive communication, symbolic awareness, and expectation that danger and risk are a central feature of the effective environment."[3] Wole Soyinka's *The Climate of Fear: The Quest for Dignity in a Dehumanized World* says the anxieties once focused on nuclear annihilation now have attached themselves to other ideas, especially in the post-9/11 years.[4] Corey Robin's *Fear: The History of a Political Idea* addresses concerns about international conflict and potential attacks on civilian populations. Robin also looks at the increases in public anxiety since September 11, 2001.[5]

It's important to stress that despite the cloud of confusion in the public generated by post-9/11 media, these broad social anxieties were well in place before those events. In 1999 Zygmunt Bauman eloquently wrote of the growing mood of "uncertainty, insecurity, and unsafety" in contemporary society.[6] Increasingly, people feel abandoned by public institutions and deceived by corporations. The majority hate their leaders yet never vote. Some would call this a postmodern moment in which the monolithic certainties of an earlier era have been thrown into question. As once dominant formulations of male authority and the nuclear family give way, the nation state is undermined by the rise of multinational capitalism. The anxieties produced by these changes are soothed by media narratives of a fantasized return to origins.

Think about all of the disappointments and reasons people have to be worried about once stable public symbols. From America's failure in Vietnam to the nation's shame over Nixon's resignation to the Reagan administration's Iran–Contra problem to the exploits of Bill Clinton – people have had good reason to lose faith in the presidency. Religion hasn't fared much better, with sex scandals in the Catholic Church and the hysteria of US religious hardliners. Corporate misbehavior and greed reached such proportions that Congress, after much arm-twisting, passed the Sarbanes/Oxley bill to throw CEOs in jail. Celebrities haven't fared well either. Consider Martha Stewart, Rush Limbaugh, William Bennett, Michael Jackson and a host of other less pious public figures who fell for vices ranging from drug abuse to child molestation. Of course the favorite targets have always been African American men. Think of O. J., Kobe, and Michael – guilty or innocent – put up for public pillory. It's been a sad era for role models.

Then there is the economy. The long-term outlook isn't good. Average Americans don't need to be told that their money is buying less, good jobs are harder to find, and that much of what they put on their backs, drive, and listen to is made in the growing economic powerhouse that is Asia. As the gap between rich and poor continues to widen in Western nations, countries in Africa and parts of Asia and Latin America fall further into misery and despair. And it isn't someone else's problem when billions of people are hungry and diseased because extremist factions in these nations are growing increasingly angry about the global imbalance in power and resources. Although the United States and its allies may say that they don't believe it, desperate people around the world hoping for a day of reckoning are finding common cause in their hatred of nations that callously exploit the rest of the world. After all, that was the real message delivered by the bombings in New York, Madrid, London, and scores of lesser-known locations throughout Iraq, Afghanistan, and other nations. People in industrialized nations have every reason to be nervous that the intensity of such attacks will only increase as their governments continue to ignore the reasons they occur.

The language of capitalism is desire. It begins with the need for simple things like food, clothing, and shelter and ends with a craving for Godiva chocolate and Gucci jeans. Contemporary society confuses what it *needs* with what it wants. People need the basic things in life: enough to put on the table, clothes to get you through the day, a place to go home to where it's warm and safe, and friends and a loving family. But the world of advertising and the media we consume convinces us and the people around us that to be satisfied in life – to really live – requires things that cost a lot of money. That old Corolla is fine, but what you really want is a new Benz or Carrera.

Fear and Desire

Theorists thought for a long time that people became convinced that they wanted certain things or needed to behave in certain ways through a process known as "false consciousness."[7] In other words, the unsuspecting "masses" could be sold a bill of goods by unscrupulous advertisers or politicians and that society operated by a huge process of propaganda. But that didn't give people much credit for independent thinking and it assumed that people's only real desires were those they were tricked into having. In the 1970s a new set of theories came along that looked at things slightly differently. Maybe ideology didn't give people new ideas about what they wanted, but instead latched onto things people really valued – like love, friendship, and safety – and convinced them that they could get these things only by behaving in certain ways or buying the right things.[8] This was the real genius of modern capitalism. It got people to believe that the road to happiness lay in material possessions and superficial signs of success. This process of ideology is what makes the consuming part of identity work. You think you need to have the right car or the right clothes to look good and be admired. And who doesn't want to look good and be admired? There's nothing really wrong with it.

How did consumer demand for purchases get so out of control? Juliet B. Schor cites what she terms the escalating "work and speed" cycle. According to Schor the American work week has expanded at the same time that public demand for commodities has grown. People work harder and longer and they want more for their efforts. To Schor these desires are fed by vastly increased exposure to advertising, much – but not all – of it on television.

> Heavy viewing has also resulted in historically unprecedented exposure to commercials. And ads have proliferated far beyond the television screen to virtually every social institution and type of public space, from museums to zoos, to college campuses and elementary school classrooms, restaurant bathrooms and menus, at the airport, and even the sky.[9]

The cruel part of contemporary marketing is that it tells you that if you can't afford to buy those things you're out of luck. And it doesn't stop with small things. This is where it gets really bad. Looking good isn't just an arbitrary set of rules that got put in place by some process of natural selection. The rules of looking good are not accidental. Somebody made them up: not one person nor even a group of corporate fat cats sitting around in a boardroom. They evolved over time in response to the dominant groups in Western society and what those groups thought was important. In the United States and Britain and much of Europe this meant white or light-skinned people in societies governed by men, heterosexual men. If you look through fashion magazines – or any magazines for that matter – you'll see ads promoting a certain kind of beauty. It's a beauty of thin, clear-skinned, young white women with enough money to buy clothes and make-up and great hair. It's a beauty that leaves out anyone who has a black, brown, or yellow complexion, as well as any woman who is big, or poor, or over 30. So in this way the message sent out by the contemporary beauty and fashion industry is one that is racist, classist, ageist, and degrading to anyone who doesn't fit its profile. And most women don't fit its profile.

Occasional efforts are made in the media industries to reverse these trends. *Marie Claire* editor Liz Jones attempted in 2000 to launch initiatives to encourage magazine editors to feature a wider diversity of women, specifically calling for models of different physical proportions and more

African American and Asian American women. Her efforts were rejected by the industry and Jones resigned from *Marie Claire* in 2001, stating "I had simply had enough of working in an industry that pretends to support women while it bombards them with impossible images of perfection day-after-day, undermining their self-confidence, their health, their hard-earned cash."[10]

The same basic set of rules applies to men. But here we can discuss behavior as well as looks. Sure, men are told that they too need to look right and have the right clothes. But with men the emphasis is placed a little more on having an impressive car and other things that show they have enough money or are smart enough to get it. But the media image of men these days also tells them that they have to be tough in certain ways. And this is where violence comes in. Many contemporary television shows, movies, and video games tell a man he needs to be able to use force, to fight, and that fighting is a suitable way to solve problems or get what you want in certain situations. This is one of the areas where media violence really does shape people's thinking in certain ways. It works in the background, in our unconscious minds, making subtle changes in our attitudes about the world and how we behave. Of course, there is a broader context that helps media violence do this. TV shows, movies, and games are by no means the whole story.

It's also important to acknowledge that the effects of media stereotypes and media violence are never absolute. Critically minded viewers continually question and contest what they see. Even the most regressive programming can contain positive elements. Lara Croft may be a hypersexualized, cartoon-like image of unattainable physical proportions, but she also represents strength, courage, and ethical responsibility in the eyes of her fans. As David Gauntlett writes, "Rather than being the object of desire who inspires the hero to action, Lara Croft is the hero, driving the story forward on her own, and reserving the right to eye certain men with desire."[11]

Gender and Race

Representations of gender and race in violent media vary by genre and media. Consider the growth of the "violent spectacle" movie genre, which emerged in the late 1960s following the revision of the industry Production Code. Straightforward action or "buddy" films evolved over time into highly stylized, special effects-driven extravaganzas typified by the overwhelming pyrotechnics of movies like *Independence Day*, *True Lies*, and the *Terminator* series. Such works are produced largely by men for male audiences who revel in the film's hyperbolic celebrations of male power and brutality. Keep in mind that women constitute a majority in the US population and a majority of overall media-viewing audiences. Yet, entertainment industry statistics bear out disparities in gender representation. Overall, women comprised 17 percent of executive producers, producers, directors, writers, cinematographers, and editors working on the top 250 films released in 2003. Women were cast in 38 percent of roles that year. Women were but 21.3 percent of news directors at television stations in 2004.[12] That same year women reported 35 percent of stories on ABC, CBS, and NBC. The physical appearance of protagonists has been marked in recent years by an increased preference for the type of overdeveloped physique typified by Sylvester Stallone, Arnold Schwarzenegger, and The Rock. It goes without saying that women characters in these films nearly always appear as victims, sex objects, or villains. As a genre, violent spectacles support the misogynistic "backlash" against women identified in 1990 by Susan Faludi and typified elsewhere in the culture by the reactionary "politically incorrect" rhetoric of media personalities like Tom Leykis and Howard Stern.[13]

This is not to say that all violent movies and television programs operate in exactly the same way. Works in contemporary horror and slasher genres that mostly feature mutilation and murder of women, usually contain elements of subversion via the triumph of a woman character in the end. Another variation in recent years is the introduction of uncertainty, vulnerability, or neurosis into otherwise macho roles in movies like *Analyze This* (1999) and *Analyze That* (2004), and TV series like *The Sopranos*. Also, audiences don't always buy into the negative portrayals they see. Viewers can exert considerable autonomy in their interpretations of characters. In *Panic Room* (2002) Jodie Foster plays a woman subjected to a home invasion. The Foster character can be read as either a victim or a hero who struggles against her assailants. In recent Asian martial arts movies like *Crouching Tiger, Hidden Dragon* (2000), and *Hero* (2003), the protagonists played by Ziyi Zhang might be seen either as sexualized objects or resistant subjects in the narrative. Moreover, many women viewers enjoy violent fare – even works that portray violence against women like slasher films or shows like the *Sopranos* and *Law and Order: SVU*. Critics such as E. Ann Kaplan and Kaja Silverman have written about the complexities of "female spectatorship" and the difficulty of ascribing pleasures of viewing directly along gender lines. These scholars assert that biological differences between men and women are merely a starting point in determining their subsequent identities and preferences. Judith Butler has theorized that adult gender identities are really more of a "performance" than a fixed or permanent state.[14] In this view an individual might put on a dress to "feel like a woman" or posture like a tough guy to "look like a man."

More self-critical in their portrayal of gender are "angry white man" films that make explicit the implicit ethnocentrism of violent spectacles. Movies from *Raging Bull* (1980) to *Falling Down* (1992) depict white protagonists beset by minorities and criminals in a world in which the foundations of the old social order are crumbling. Here, as in almost all crime and war movies, people of color play the role of a deviant "other." This is most pronounced in the treatment of women characters. A study conducted by Robert Entman and Andrew Rojecki in 1996 found African American women committing physical violence in 56 percent of movies, as opposed to 11 percent for white women. Black female characters were restrained in 55 percent, in comparison to 6 percent for whites. Black women used obscenities in 89 percent of the movies, while white women did so in but 17 percent.[15]

Despite countless critiques of the ubiquitous racism of the television industry, little change has occurred aside from occasional token gestures or cynical appeals to "ethnic" niche markets. In 1999 the National Association for the Advancement of Colored People (NAACP) threatened a boycott of the major television networks over their negative portrayals of minorities and their exclusionary hiring policies. NAACP president and CEO Kweisi Mfume termed the year's fall lineup a "virtual whitewash" in its failure to cast a single person of color in a major role in any of its 26 new series. Perhaps the most pernicious racism in violent media appears in science fiction films, where the other becomes a menacing "alien." From the casting of James Earl Jones as Darth Vader to the villainous portrayals by minorities in *The Arrival* (1996), *They Live* (1996), and *Independence Day* (1996) – not white means not human. As explained by Lianne McCarty,

> In *Independence Day* this association between human and white is made from the onset in the shot of the US flag on the moon and the monument inscribed: "Here men from the planet earth first set foot upon the moon. We come in peace for all mankind." Whiteness is simultaneously disavowed (nowhere) – its specificity unacknowledged – and universalized (everywhere) – made to stand in for all "mankind."[16]

René Girard, one of the leading theorists on violence, asserts that societies rely on villains for social coherence. People become unified through a common "scapegoat" they all can hate or fear. Girard states:

By a scapegoat effect I mean that strange process through which two or more people are reconciled at the expense of a third party who appears guilty or responsible for whatever ails, disturbs, or frightens the scapegoaters. They feel relieved of their tensions and they coalesce into a more harmonious group. They now have a single purpose.[17]

Of course, the selection of the scapegoat is never an innocent process. It is informed by the understandings and beliefs of the particular society. The United States has relied heavily on scapegoats since its founding. Although it's common to think of scapegoating in terms of ethnic stereotyping, movies and television have frequently used nationality as a way to generalize about groups. In his book *Imagined Communities*, Benedict Anderson stated that nationalism is like an older sibling to ethnicity and race.[18] From the pioneer days of what Richard Slotkin has termed the "gunfighter nation," the US has been defined by unity and exclusion.[19] A unified America stands in opposition to the external "other" that helps define the US in terms of what lies outside of it.[20] The formulation of the monomyth is easy in times of war, as evidenced in film and print depictions of the Japanese and Germans during World War II. According to Slotkin, when a clear external scapegoat is missing others must be found to allow the national "regeneration through violence."[21]

In the current era, US news media cast certain groups in the scapegoat role: immigrants, people of color, the homeless, and the poor. These groups continue to be portrayed as lawbreakers in movie and television crime dramas far in excess of their representation in the population. As Elayne Rapping writes, "the crime drama delineates the symbolic geography within which social order must be maintained; the political imagination within which endless rituals of social disruption and return to harmony and peace are performed."[22] In this way programs like *Law and Order*, *Homicide*, and *The Wire* explicate the separation of right and wrong, deviant and normal behavior, legal and illegal. Reinforced by news reporting that is often indistinguishable from entertainment programming, this violent logic becomes internalized by the society, as it must for a democracy to continue to use violence. This is how violence is publicly authorized. Barbara Whitmer states that "what distinguishes violence from power, strength, force, and authority is its instrumental character. As a phenomenon, violence is closest to strength." Whitmer concludes that "the means of violence, like other tools, are designed to multiply natural strength until they eventually can be substituted for it."[23]

Crime and Politics

Representations of violence play an important role in the legitimization of police and military action. Drama and news programs provide endlessly repeated narratives of threats or of violence that demands counterviolence sanctioned by the citizenry. Once the leading nation in the production and distribution of violent media, the United States remains the world leader in the commission of state-sanctioned violence.[24] The US is the only Western nation to use the death penalty; 73.4 percent of its citizens support the policy.[25] As rates of violent crime have gradually decreased during the past decade, prison construction has become the nation's fastest-growing industry.[26] Of the two million people incarcerated in the US, half are African American and 70 percent are illiterate.[27] Is it merely coincidence that the majority of criminals depicted in movies and television programs are people of color?

Obviously, media violence does not create these circumstances. But constant exposure to stories of violent crime creates an environment of suggestibility. In the 1930s Walter Lippman wrote in his classic book *Public Opinion* that people cannot gather from direct experience the information they need to function as citizens in a democratic society. They rely on various kinds of media to form their opinions. Today 76 percent of Americans say that they base their perceptions about crime on what they see on TV and read in the newspaper.[28] This leads to regrettable misconceptions. The coverage of crime in the news does not correspond with the occurrence of crime in society. As Lori Dorfman and Vincent Schiraldi write:

> Violent crime dominates crime coverage. Crime is often the dominant topic on local television news, network news, and TV news magazines. In general, TV crime reporting is the inverse of crime frequency. That is, murder is reported most often on news though it happens the least. Several analyses of evening news found that, although homicides made up from two-tenths of one percent of all arrests, homicides made up more than a quarter (25–27 percent) of crimes reported on the news.[29]

Even as crime rates have decreased, coverage of crime has increased. Between 1990 and 1998, national crime rates fell by 20 percent, as network television showed an 83 percent increase in crime news.[30] Homicide coverage rose by 473 percent as homicides declined by 33 percent.[31]

The reasons for these disparities between fact and fiction are economic in part. As television networks and movie studios become subsidiaries of multinational conglomerates, pressure has grown to deliver profits. News programs compete with each other and with entertainment programs for viewers. As a consequence they become splashier and more oriented toward the spectacular. The effects of this sensational-ization are hardly neutral. They create an atmosphere that enabled California's passage in 1994 of voter initiative Proposition 184, the nation's first "Three Strikes" law. The law was established shortly after the widely publicized abduction and murder of 8-year-old Polly Klaas and the crusade-like media campaign for the law led by the child's father. In the summer of 2002 the powerful effect of stories about victimized children led to the implementation of a system of statewide media alerts reminiscent of air-raid warnings. This occurred despite a decline in child abductions.

Without a doubt, the culture of fear that results from the misrepresenta-tion of threats to the public creates an ugly situation. But it does something more. It sets up a tempting opportunity for politicians anxious to please voters or to get government to take certain actions. Someone running for office can get the support of anxious voters by promising to hire more police or make the army stronger. For this kind of election campaign, it's helpful in a cynical kind of way for people to be frightened or to think they are in danger. People running for office throughout the history of the United States and in other countries have used public worries about crime, or immigration, or threats from other countries to convince voters that they were the right candidates for the jobs. As you might expect, it's been an effective strategy and one that's a lot easier to use than making a case for getting elected on issues like the environment or employment.

The practice of using threats of violence to manipulate politics has been in the news quite a bit in the recent decade, especially in the United States. In domestic politics it came up during the 1980s and 1990s in California and in certain states along the Mexican border when a number of polit-icians began to blame rising rates of unemployment, welfare dependency, and educational failure on illegal immigrants entering the US from the south. Throughout 2006 the US Congress and President Bush argued for months over the nation's use of Mexican immigrants. This led to tighter border controls and the passage of harsh laws to punish undocumented workers discovered in the US – even though the economies of those states heavily depended on the willingness of the illegals to do difficult work for low wages. Eventually it became evident that the economic and social problems were not caused by immigrants and many of the laws were repealed.

This propagation of misinformation has even more profound effects for foreign policy and defense. These are areas considerably more removed from people's lived experience than crime and hence even more contingent on media representation. In these areas the federal government now literally writes the news. A secondary effect of the monetary squeeze on network news departments has been the virtual elimination of investigatory journalism. Although much was made of governmental media manipulation during the 1992 Desert Storm offensive, television had for some years already capitulated to the Pentagon and White House information offices in its near total reliance on them for government-related content. Regardless of one's opinion about the war on terrorism, there is little doubt that public knowledge about the campaign is limited to what Washington releases. This is done because war is the ultimate example of rationalized state violence. To gain public consent for war its stakes must be raised to the level of myth and history.

In the discourse of media violence no figure of otherness surpasses that of the terrorist. Writing in 1999 Elayne Rapping argued that "terrorists are portrayed as irrational, inscrutable, and inherently violent. They threaten to infiltrate our porous border, bringing with them fear, chaos, and disorder."[32] This creates the impression that terrorists can't be rehabilitated because they cannot be reconciled with our system of logic and justice. Framing terrorists in this way encourages the establishment of more powerful methods of law enforcement and incarceration because terrorists cannot recognize or comprehend standard means. To Rapping,

> terrorists are marked in the media by dramatic signs of difference, physical and psychological. These signs are so repellant and horrifying that they easily justify the use of measures previously unthinkable in the enforcement of "normal" criminal law, because terrorists are not "normal" criminals; they are alien, inhuman monsters.[33]

These remarks remind us that the reactions of the Bush administration, regarded by some as cynically theatrical and politically opportunistic, have deeper roots in past events. But network news rarely provides much depth or historical perspective. Connections rarely are made with the prior three decades of terrorist assaults on US holdings – not to mention the sponsorship or direct execution of terrorism by the US in places like Afghanistan, Angola, China, Indonesia, Lebanon, Russia, Sudan, Syria, Turkey, and Vietnam. The difference is that recent assaults have been on American soil – and that was exactly their point.

The War on Terrorism

September 11 provided the penultimate example of media violence. The stories and famous footage of the World Trade Center towers collapsing occupied all of the major networks for four straight days, during which all other programming was suspended. Much is made of the uniqueness of the moment – of the way September 11 "forever changed" the way the US viewed itself. Introducing *The Age of Terror*, one of dozens of books to appear about September 11, John Lewis Gaddis solemnly states, "Whatever we eventually settle on calling the events of September 11 – the Attack on America, Black Tuesday, 9/11 – they've already forced a reconsideration, not only of where we are as a nation and where we might be going, but also of where we've been, even who we are."[34]

While it is emotionally satisfying to dwell on the exceptional scale of the assaults, much of the discourse seemed oddly familiar. This is because the entertainment industry had already depicted fictional events so similar to the September 11 attack that many viewers remarked how "like a movie" the footage seemed. Adopting familiar motifs, news coverage wrote a violent narrative of good versus evil and us versus them – complete with a nefarious "evil doer" of a leader. The novelty of the assaults created an atmosphere devoid of any criticality whatsoever, due in large part to the networks' fear that the appearance of an "unpatriotic" opinion would mean lost advertising revenue. This has produced an atmosphere in which alternative perspectives were rarely reported, and as a consequence rarely debated in public. This meant that those seeking a range of opinion had to look elsewhere. The good news has been that the topic of terrorism has become a huge internet phenomenon, with hundreds of sites providing divergent perspectives. In a similar fashion, the post-9/11 tunnel vision of mainstream news has enlivened independent publishing and media production. People are looking to alternative media and the internet with an urgency missing before the attacks.

Ultimately this broadening of the discourse is the answer to the larger media violence dilemma. The problem isn't that we have too much violence in movies and TV. The problem is that the kind of violence portrayed is so limited. Due to the consolidation of production into the hands of a few giant multinational corporations, decision making is conducted by a small number of executives who are mostly white, mostly male, and driven by the need to make a profit. This economic imperative to reach huge audiences through extremely polished and expensive programs eliminates the willingness to take risks or to deviate from proven formulas. So we get violent media of a very particular kind – anesthetized to maximize its accessibility and its capacity to stimulate viewers – and endlessly repeated stories of male strength and good old fashioned American power. And it really isn't hurting anyone that much, at least not directly. Instead it's doing something much more pernicious. The mass production of media violence is wasting an enormous resource that might otherwise be capable of tremendous public good. People learn about the world and form their understandings of it to a great extent from public culture. They gather from it the material they need to function as citizens and to participate in the democratic process. The reduction of the nation's media discourse to a redundant series of violent spectacles does something much worse than teaching people to become aggressive. It tells them to do nothing.

4

We Can't Stop the Violence: The Uses and Importance of Media Violence

Media violence is here to stay. There's no getting around it. One of the biggest misperceptions in the media violence debate is that somehow there might be a way someday to do away with it – through legislation, market regulation, consumer boycotting, or giant campaigns to "just say no" or "turn off your TV." The problem is that violence is just too ingrained in our culture to eliminate. Some would even say that it is a part of human nature or embedded in our psychological make-up so deeply that we can't root it out. And while it's important to question people who suggest that mundane violence is "just a part of life" and that certain kinds of violence just come naturally to some people, it's equally foolish to think that we can wipe aggression and its representations away completely. We wouldn't want to if we could, because it would mean removing a part of what makes us human – like it or not. And besides, there's a gigantic social and economic infrastructure that's built, in part, on violence, the threat of violence, the legally sanctioned violence that law enforcement uses to protect us, and the capacities for military violence that maintain the world order most of the time.

Violence and Education

There are plenty of reasons that people want to look at violence. Some of them are educational. It's important for children to know that human history has a violent past. Tribes and civilizations have grown up in conflict. Global commerce and colonization often utilized violent means to accomplish their goals. Battles have been fought to defend territorial boundaries or in the interest of expanding territory, rightly or wrongly. It is often argued these days that violent means are required to maintain the peace. Indeed it was the threat of "mutually assured destruction" that for decades kept the great nuclear powers in a period of peace or *détente* following World War II. Like certain terms of hate speech, it would be impossible and unadvisable to remove violence from the lexicon of human history. Besides, we learn from past mistakes. Just because a people have had a violent history doesn't mean it must have a violent future. Knowing, representing, and teaching about violence and peace can help us make a better world.

The lessons of historical violence have been written down and visualized in enduring works of literature and art. These stories, books, paintings, and works of sculpture are found in libraries and museums around the world. In many cases they stand as testimony to the men and women who sacrificed their lives in the name of justice and freedom. Freedom is a good thing. It's one of those words that gets bandied about a great deal by people who want to use it to advance their own agendas. But in the end it remains an important human value worth fighting for. And many generations of people in many nations have paid dearly for it. Sometimes these sacrifices are memorialized in monuments to help people remember lessons from the past. In the United States the Vietnam Veterans Memorial Wall in Washington, DC was designed by an Asian American design student named Maya Lin. The Wall, as it is known, is dedicated to honoring those who died in the Vietnam War. Since it was first dedicated in 1976 it has evolved into something more. It is now also a place of healing for those affected by one of the most divisive wars in the nation's history. So representations of violence can be important.

The Nazi Holocaust is another widely memorialized human tragedy. The Holocaust was the systematic, bureaucratic, state-sponsored persecution and murder of approximately six million Jews by the Nazi regime and its collaborators. "Holocaust" is a word of Greek origin meaning "sacrifice by fire." The Nazis, who came to power in Germany in January 1933, believed that Germans were "racially superior" and that the Jews, deemed "inferior," were "life unworthy of life."[1] During the era of the Holocaust, the Nazis also targeted other groups because of their perceived "racial inferiority": Roma (Gypsies), the handicapped, and some of the Slavic peoples (Poles, Russians, and others). Other groups were persecuted on political and behavioral grounds, among them communists, socialists, Jehovah's Witnesses, and homosexuals.

Learning about the history of the Holocaust encourages people to reflect upon moral and ethical questions and upon their responsibilities as citizens of a democracy. Studying the history of the Holocaust can promote an understanding of prejudice, racism, and stereotyping in any society while raising questions of fairness, justice, individual identity, peer pressure, conformity, indifference, and obedience. Exposure to appropriate representations of the violence of the Holocaust can enhance understanding of the Holocaust and related issues, including contemporary examples of genocide.

Steven Spielberg's *Schindler's List* (1993) is often held up as an example of contemporary movie making used to teach audiences about the horrors of the Nazi holocaust. In the movie Spielberg brought his filmmaking abilities to bear on this terrible story. But in at least one instance even Spielberg was unable to use his storytelling skills to move viewers in appropriate ways. *Schindler's List* is the based-on-truth story of Nazi Czech businessman Oskar Schindler, who uses Jewish labor to start a factory in occupied Poland. As World War II progresses, and the fate of the Jews becomes more and more clear, Schindler's motivations switch from profit to human sympathy and he is able to save over 1,100 Jews from death in the gas chambers.[2] In *Schindler's List*, Spielberg portrays a number of scenes of Nazis executing prisoners with an intensity intended to shock viewers into sympathy with the Jewish victims of the Holocaust. In one scene a Nazi soldier kills a Jewish woman working on the construction of a building in a concentration camp. Spielberg shows the soldier and the woman speaking at length before showing the soldier killing the woman. His intention was to heighten the emotional impact of the moment, depicting the incident without a cut in the editing of the scene.[3] He certainly never intended the scene to be funny in any way or to make people laugh. But that is exactly what happened at one, now famous, screening in Oakland, California. A group of high-school students were out on a field trip on Martin Luther King Day, when school was closed. As the movie reached the execution scene, the students laughed, leading to requests from other people seeing the movie for the 70 students to be removed from the theater. The students said that they hadn't intended to express racism or anti-Semitism and that they always laughed and talked when they went to the movies. They simply thought the way the woman fell was funny. While it is possible that the students were simply uncomfortable with the subject matter or that they didn't want their peers to know they were feeling empathy with the characters, the incident shows how even when filmmakers intend to use violence to educate people, it can backfire, making a joke of a serious moment.

It would be impossible to tell the story of civilization without recounting the violence and loss of life that took place in the wars and battles of human history. Many of these conflicts occurred for important reasons and the struggles they represent need to be remembered because lessons can continue to be taken from them. For people living in the United States, for example, it remains important to remember the reasons for that nation's Revolutionary War. Several factors contributed to the Revolution. Most American settlers were motivated by a conviction that they were entitled to the full democratic rights of the British. The British believed that the colonies were to be used and exploited in whatever way suited Great Britain. That made war inevitable. The British were planning a surprise attack on Lexington, where arms were stored, and Paul Revere discovered the British plans. One night, Revere rode out to warn colonial militia of the approaching British. With this advance warning, the militiamen fought 800 British troops on April 19, 1775. The battle broke out at Concord and the Revolutionary War began.

Stories like this are important. They give people a sense of pride in their history and origins. And the stories often contain violent details that need to be included to convey the whole significance of the events. World War I tore Europe apart and many people died. The first shots of World War I occurred near a small Belgian village in August 1914. The war would last four years and ultimately cost millions of lives. At the time reports had been received that large numbers of German troops were moving into Belgium. A British squadron of about 200 men was dispatched to Belgium to see what was happening. A brief skirmish occurred that led to many famous battles. The background behind the war remains in dispute. Under Kaiser Wilhelm II, Germany moved from a policy to maintain peace with its neighbors to a more aggressive stance. It declined to renew a treaty with Russia, choosing instead to align with Austro-Hungary, Germany's eastern neighbor. France and Russia signed their own alliance in 1894, and were later joined by the British. After the assassination of its heir in 1914, the Austro-Hungarian Empire attacked Serbia, knowing Germany would support it. The actual fighting started with the invasion of Belgium, with Germany taking parts of Belgium, France, Poland, and Russia. Eventually the Allies that included many European countries and the United States defeated Germany.

The legacy of World War I would later cause the eruption of World War II in Europe, Africa, and the Pacific. World War I also set in motion many of the problems the world is now facing in the Middle East. The countries we know as Egypt, Iran, Iraq, Israel, Jordan, Syria, Turkey, and numerous others were at the turn of the century all part of the Ottoman Empire, the world's greatest independent Islamic power. Impressed by the German expansion in Europe, the Ottoman Empire saw World War I as a way to regain lost lands and to expand its own reach, and it formed an alliance with Germany in the war. The British feared that the Ottomans might decide to cut off supplies of oil supplying the British Navy through the Anglo-Persian pipeline and decided with the help of India to invade the Ottomans at the coastal city of Basra, Iraq. The Ottomans decided to strike back by assaulting the Suez Canal in Egypt but failed. Meanwhile, the British and Indian armies swept across Iraq to Baghdad. Then British and Indian armies swept from their positions in Egypt to defeat Turkey and invaded and conquered Palestine. When the British took Jerusalem in 1917 they were the first Christian forces to conquer the holy city since the crusades, when Christians had taken the Holy Lands from Muslims between the eleventh and the fourteenth centuries.

Violence and Art

Learning about this history and the violence it entailed helps us understand our past and provides insight on violent conflicts taking place today. No one would deny the importance of appropriate representations of such violence in books, images, films, and television programs – difficult and painful as they may be in evoking the terrible memories of these conflicts. The same case can be made for representations of any war or even records of historically significant natural disasters, crimes, or other human tragedies. Occurrences of violence have often been the inspiration or subject matter of important works of literature or art. Enduring works from every culture in the world frequently depict horrific representations of hunts, battles, murders, fires, accidents, or post-mortem remains. The art of the Western world is especially prone to violent imagery, so much so that its very history is often framed in relation to the violent circumstances that defined the major epochs of Western civilization.

Why does that violence figure so prominently in great works of art? Cultural critic Susan Sontag wrote that the human appetite for pictures of violence and pain is nearly as universal as that for naked bodies.[4] For centuries Christian art offered up images such as those of John the Baptist being decapitated or Jesus crucified on the cross with never a question raised about the appropriateness of such gruesome imagery. Sontag suggested, as many others have, that people take a certain satisfaction from looking at such pictures without flinching. They get pleasure from knowing they can take it. And they also get another kind of satisfaction when they do flinch.

The Oxford History of Western Art, one of the most respected canonical works in the discipline of art history, divides the progression of Western culture into five periods, each one punctuated by a violent upheaval or war.[5] As stated in the volume's introduction,

> Three of the big dividing points – the fall of Classical Rome in 410, the sack of Papal Rome in 1527, and the start of the First World War in 1914 – could serve as markers in many branches of Western history, while the fourth, 1770, has been chosen to mark the start of two decades that saw a series of revolutionary transformations, most notably American Independence and the French Revolution.[6]

Not only are the separations between the art-historical periods marked by violent conflict, but a recurrent theme in Western art history is violent destruction or theft of art itself by conquering nations and peoples. The demarcation between Greek and Roman culture was underscored from the third century BC as the Romans expanded into southern Italy, Sicily, and finally into Greece – looting Greek sculpture and distributing it among wealthy Romans eager to show off Hellenic artifacts as status symbols. Rome would itself be overrun several hundred years later by the Visigoths, with the city and much of its cultural grandeur reduced to ruins.

The classical sculpture of ancient Greece most frequently depicted idealized representations of the human body. The male nude was Greek sculpture's central genre, beginning with the *kouros* and the warrior in the fifth century BC. Vases and wall paintings of the age commemorated heroic scenes of hunting and combat, as well as mythological conflicts. Roman sculpture of the first century AD included relief sculptures – or friezes – of armies charging into battle. The earliest preserved Roman paintings, found on third- to second-century tombs, are pictures of military exploits celebrating the fortunes of war.[7] For example, the *Alexander Mosaic* (second century BC) from the House of the Faun, Pompeii, depicts a gruesome battle scene with dozens of combatants on horses. Men are shown fighting with swords and whips, some trampled and impaled with spears. One of the ironies of such works lies in their ability both to document horrific moments in history and to function as beautiful pieces of art. Later critics would reflect upon how these two processes of representation work together as one.

In many religions violent imagery holds a central, even sacred, place. Anyone who has seen Mel Gibson's *The Passion of the Christ* (2004) knows that depictions of religious history can be powerful. Early Christian artworks illustrated biblical stories in illuminated manuscripts and stained glass windows of cathedrals. Sometimes these showed scenes of the martyrdom and suffering of saints. Other Christian artworks depicted the horrors of the crusades. The most common subject, of course, was Jesus, whose crucifixion and death provided endless inspiration for artists for hundreds of years.

European neoclassicism in the eighteenth century retained the Greco-Roman appetite for images of war and conquest. The French painter Jacques-Louis David often drew inspiration from the legendary history of the Early Roman Republic. In Italy, Titian (Tiziano Vecellio) painted scenes of mythological conflict. Caravaggio was known for the realism of his religious paintings. In France, the history painting of Nicolas Poussin portrayed the gruesome details of war. Poussin's *Death of Germanicus* (1627) shows the warrior in his bed succumbing to a cup of poison given to him by a servant of his stepfather Tiberius. Germanicus is surrounded by his grief-stricken family and by Roman soldiers, heavily armed and ready to avenge his impending death. Many Dutch and Flemish painters of the period expressed dramatic religiosity in response to growing Protestant patronage of artists. Rembrandt van Rijn, Anthony van Dyck, and Peter Paul Rubens also accepted commissions from the Catholic Church. Typical of this work is Rubens's *The Descent from the Cross* (1616–17), showing the lifeless body of Jesus being lowered into the arms of his followers, his abdomen torn open and still bleeding from a wound inflicted during the Crucifixion. Meanwhile, painters like Albert Eckhout and Benjamin West in the North American settlements were depicting scenes of military violence and bloodshed often involving native peoples.

Then came the art of the revolutionary wars in France and the United States and a succession of eighteenth-century history painters including Antoine-Jean Gros, Joseph Mallord William Turner, Théodore Géricault, and Francisco de Goya y Lucientes. Even before the revolutionary wars and the Napoleonic campaigns, a preoccupation with human mortality had become apparent in European art. Parisian officials in the 1780s became distressed by a growing public taste for "black subjects" that they feared would lead to moral decay.[8] Géricault's painting *Severed Limbs* (1818) is a case in point, depicting amputated hands and feet in chiaroscuro light. Goya is famous for his paintings that both documented and criticized political violence. Goya's series *Los Desastres de la Guerra* (The disasters of war) (1810–20), depicting French soldiers killing peasants, stands as one of the most dramatic statements protesting the horrors of war by an artist during this period. The earliest of such anti-war artworks were a group of etchings made in 1633 by Jacques Callot. Titled *Les Misères et malheurs de la guerre* (The miseries and misfortunes of war), the images depicted atrocities committed against civilians during the invasion of Lorraine in the early 1630s.

Public sculpture has often memorialized armed conflict and violence. Almost every nation has civic monuments commemorating great military victories and honoring those who died in wars. Napoleon I used sculptors to publicize his image as an undefeatable military strategist and a commander of devastating forces. King Louis XVIII, like other monarchs, similarly would commission statuary of generals on horseback to reinforce ideals of heroism. Many governments created colossal monumental works during the nineteenth century in the interest of nationalistic pride, among them the US Washington Memorial and Nelson's Column in London's Trafalgar Square. The important point is that representations of mortal combat and warriors who have committed horrible violence have always been present in public life and revered in places where people gather to reflect upon their national history.

Violence and News

With the invention of photography in the mid-nineteenth century an entirely new medium was born for the presentation of violence. Early photography required long exposure times and was limited initially to still lifes, landscapes, and formal portraiture. Post-mortem portraits of the dead were made in the 1840 and 1850s using daguerreotype and ferrotype processes. But the real start of news photography took place with the Crimean War and the American Civil War. From the very beginning war photography was political. Roger Fenton, called by many the first war photographer, was sent to the Crimea in 1855 by Britain's Prince Albert. His mission was to photograph the war – but not the dead or wounded. The British wanted to counteract the terrible news of the war that was appearing in newspaper stories with photographs that showed the British army at its best. So Fenton was allowed full access to the military, which largely staged the photographs he took of them preparing to go into battle. But he never photographed the war itself.

Matthew Brady was a jewel-case maker who learned the techniques for making photographs from inventor Samuel Morse. Brady started making portraits of important people in Washington, DC, including Abraham Lincoln, and when the Civil War broke out Brady decided to record it using photography. Brady hired 23 photographers to travel throughout the country during the war with portable darkrooms so that they could develop their collodion plate pictures as they took them. Lincoln made sure that Brady's photographers could get to all of the important battles. Like Prince Albert in Britain, Lincoln wanted photographs that could be used to build support for the war effort. As historians later determined, many of the images that Brady's people made turned out to be fakes, or pictures of scenes that had been tampered with. But the Brady photographers, especially Alexander Gardner and Timothy O'Sullivan, attained great renown for their reporting. As reported in the *New York Times*,

> Mr. Brady has done something to bring home to us the terrible reality and earnestness of war. If he has not brought bodies and laid them in our door-yards and along the streets, he has done something very like it . . . These pictures have a terrible distinctness.[9]

Movies came on the scene toward the end of the century, with the first newsreel presenting the 1898 Battle of San Juan Hill during the Spanish-American War. With then Colonel Theodore Roosevelt leading his famous Rough Riders cavalry unit, the scene was staged for Vitagraph cameramen after the actual fighting had taken place, because the original battle had been deemed insufficiently dramatic for movie making.

War photography became contentious during World War I when both the French and German high commands banned pictures taken by all except a few selected military photographers.[10] As in other conflicts, warring governments understood the importance of controlling the information their citizens received so that support for fighting could be maximized. War often has been an endeavor that has needed encouragement among the populations called upon to supply young people who were likely to be killed in the fighting. And there always have been opponents to war. One of the first photographic critiques of war appeared in Germany in 1924. In a book entitled *Krieg dem Kriege!* (*War against War!*) Ernst Friedrich presented a sequence of photographs that begins with images of toy soldiers and then continues with progressive intensity to depict the devastation and, eventually, the human carnage wrought by the fighting in World War I. *War against War!* proved enormously popular throughout Europe and sold ten editions by 1930.

Violent imagery found its first genuine outlet of mass circulation with the introduction of weekly magazines later in the decade, specifically *Life Magazine* (1936) in the US and *Picture Post* (1938) in the United Kingdom. Both magazines featured grizzly pictures of the Spanish Civil War in their early years of publication, with one typical headline proclaiming, "*Life's* camera gets closer to Spanish war than any camera has ever got before."[11] Innovations in camera technology also played a role in the broadened circulation of war imagery. The introduction of the German Leica 35mm camera in 1925 gave photographers a smaller, lighter camera with quick shutter speeds and the ability to take dozens of pictures without changing films. This gave photojournalists a mobility that enabled the type of action pictures of battle that made photographers like Robert Capa famous. Capa's brand of photojournalism hit its stride during World War II, as the public's appetite for war imagery demanded pictures from the front lines. As in prior conflicts, the hunger for images that struck the appropriate nationalistic notes sometimes tempted photographers to take liberties with their subject matter. Such was the case with the famous photograph by Joe Rosenthal of the raising of the American flag on Iwo Jima in 1945. The dramatic image of US Marines triumphantly planting the flag atop Mount Suribachi at the culmination of a furious battle, in fact, had been staged hours after the fighting had ceased – when a larger flag could be substituted for the original to create a more photogenic scene.

Vietnam was the first televised war and the first war in US history that elicited massive national protest. Never before had the horrors of armed conflict been presented to the US public – or any news audience – in such a graphic and relentless fashion. Day after day in the 1960s and into the 1970s, the American public saw television footage, mostly of bombings, and received casualty counts. The violence of the Vietnam War delivered through television and news magazines made the war seem more immediate and "real" than any conflict in the past. It upset people in a way they hadn't been upset before because they had never seen war in this way before. The public knew that the photographs that came home from Vietnam could not be set-ups. The 1972 photograph, circulated throughout the world, of a naked Vietnamese girl running toward the camera in frightened tears from a village just napalmed by US planes, could never have been staged.[12] The photograph taken in 1968 by Eddie Adams of a South Vietnamese policeman executing a Vietcong suspect with a pistol shot to the head could not have been faked. During the Vietnam War almost all photojournalism came to be regarded as *de facto* criticism of US involvement in the region.[13]

Following Vietnam many governments were understandably wary of the risks of free and unrestrained access to armed conflicts by the press. During the 1982 British campaign in the Falkland Islands, Prime Minister Margaret Thatcher granted access to only two pre-selected photographers, with no television coverage permitted whatsoever. Similar lessons from Vietnam had been learned by US President George H. W. Bush. In the 1991 war in the Persian Gulf, US authorities successfully manipulated coverage to allow only highly mediated images largely photographed from war planes depicting the war as a video-game-like conflict in which human casualties were represented only as animated explosions on computer screens. The same sanitized form of coverage was used in the 2001–2 American assault on Afghanistan, which produced the impression that no US soldiers at all were being injured or killed in the fighting. As Susan Sontag has pointed out, this abstraction and distancing of armed conflict from the eyes of the American public has created the impression among many that violence and suffering are conditions that inexplicably strike only others in foreign nations far removed from US soil.[14] This is one of the reasons the terrible tragedy of the World Trade Center attacks on September 11, 2001 at first seemed so incomprehensible. The only response that many American viewers could muster on that horrible day was that the images appearing on television newscasts were somehow "just like a movie."

The Media Violence Industry

There's a longstanding chicken-and-egg debate in media violence circles that runs something like this. On one side stands the entertainment industry saying that the public's demand for violent excitement drives the market. Audiences really get a kick out of action movies, scary thrillers, first-person shooter games, and reality TV. And what's wrong with that? On the other side stand consumer advocates who say that the entertainment industry is producing dangerous products that cause people to harm themselves and others – and that the industry very cleverly stimulates desires for these products through marketing and advertising that convinces people that violent entertainment is natural, fun, and harmless – when instead what such entertainment is really doing is teaching people, especially kids, to hate and hurt and kill. Which side is right?

Let's start with the entertainment industry. If the industry believes that it is responding to consumer demand for violent entertainment, how does it determine the ways it will respond to consumer desires? One of the most familiar refrains one hears from supporters of a free-market system is that the natural laws of supply and demand determine what gets made and consumed and what doesn't. So it would seem to make sense – from the perspective of the entertainment industry – that there exists a growing demand for media violence that has been articulated and is being answered by a similarly growing supply. In other words, a logical process must be operating that culminates in the presence of so much violent material in the media environment. While it would be simplistic to think that a single set of assumptions drives all of the production, marketing, and distribution decisions across the range of movie, television, publishing, and computer game media, certain general principles have emerged over time – and gained importance in the past decade. Some of these principles that drive the media violence industry are simply extensions of business and creative practices that have been in place throughout the history of mass entertainment. Others are quite new and some are unique to recently developed (and currently developing) technologies of media production and dissemination.

The New Economics of Entertainment

Without a doubt, the single most important factor in the ongoing presence of media violence is the dramatic change that has occurred in recent decades in the economic structure of the entertainment industry. The continuing consolidation of movie, television, and publishing companies and their acquisition by large, multinational corporations has resulted in operating philosophies and business procedures unlike those of the movie studios, television networks, and publishing houses that people once knew. Gone are the days of Hollywood moguls with stables of legendary movie stars making pictures on the basis of personal taste and creative instinct. Television is no longer the province of network executives who might champion situation comedies, long-form dramatic series, or Pulitzer Prize-winning news departments. And publishing is now completely a numbers game, with boutique presses and idiosyncratic novels giving way to million-copy press runs and blockbuster titles designed for maximum exposure on television talk shows and Waldenbooks.

These media industries have been changed by an accelerating pattern of corporate mergers and acquisitions that has been occurring during the past 25 years, which gained tremendous momentum in the past decade. Actually the process began well before that – as movie studios, broadcast networks, and publishers began merging and buying one another primarily in the years following World War II. But in more recent decades, these discrete media companies have been swallowed by huge multimedia empires or acquired by gigantic corporations with little intrinsic interest in movies or television or news, but with a big interest – indeed an all-consuming mandate – in satisfying the demands of corporate investors for continuing profits. This has meant that money – not ethics, or taste, or politics – has become the driving force in entertainment and journalism. And that is one of the biggest reasons why the flow of media violence has become nearly unstoppable.

Six multinational corporations now control the major US media: Rupert Murdoch's News Corporation (FOX, HarperCollins, *New York Post*, *Weekly*

Standard, *TV Guide*, DirecTV, and 35 TV stations), General Electric (NBC, CNBC, MSNBC, Telemundo, Bravo, Universal Pictures, and 28 TV stations), Time Warner (AOL, CNN, Warner Bros., *Time* and its 130-plus magazines), Disney (ABC, Disney Channel, ESPN, 10 TV and 72 radio stations), Viacom (CBS, MTV, Nickelodeon, Paramount Pictures, Simon & Schuster, and 183 US radio stations), and Bertelsmann (Random House and its more than 120 imprints worldwide, and Gruner + Jahr and its more than 110 magazines in 10 countries).[15]

Is this consolidation of media ownership good or bad? Some people argue that bigger is better because it results in more economic muscle and greater economies of scale. These factors, it is argued, combine to reduce business operating expenses and as a consequence yield higher returns for corporate investors and lower prices for consumers – a "win-win" situation. Many of these efficiencies derive from the globalization of corporations, which allows them to sell their products around the world, decentralize the manufacture of goods, utilize labor pools in nations where people work for little money, and negotiate favorable trade relationships. The downside of all of this is that corporate consolidation, for all of its apparent benefits, often harms the very people and nations its advocates claim to be helping. This is because the corporate profits, bargain-priced goods, and great trade arrangements tend to give the most benefit to the wealthy and powerful people who run the corporations and make the deals. As a consequence the rich of the world get richer and the poor get poorer. What effect does this new economic environment have on media violence? To answer that question one needs to examine the different ways movies, television, publishing, and more recently computer games and digital media, have responded to the new money game.

The Movie Business

During the last three decades the system of exhibiting, marketing, and distributing major motion pictures has undergone a radical transformation. Also, the relationship of movies to other consumer products has changed dramatically. The story of this transformation began in the late 1960s and 1970s in changes in the ways feature films were brought to audiences. Up to this point movies were released in selected large theaters in major metropolitan cities. But by the early 1970s, movie theater companies recognized the potentials of inexpensively built multi-screen theaters in suburban and out-of-town shopping malls. Between 1969 and 1973 movie theater construction increased tenfold. Subsequently the number of movie "screens" in the US rose from 10,000 in 1975 to 22,750 in 1990.[16] More theaters created a need for more copies of movies, with "press-runs" growing from 500 prints to 8,000 or more. Advertising changed too, with regional television campaigns giving way to national network buys – which marked the beginning of national blanket release patterns for feature films. The combined effect of the expansion of theaters and national release practices meant that economic stakes for individual movies increased dramatically. It also meant that the feature film business was no longer a place for small independent companies who by themselves could not afford the costs of the new national (and soon thereafter global) movie business.

The happy part of this story – at least initially – for the motion picture industry was that sales and revenues from individual movies rose exponentially, with a few particular films breaking industry records. The success of *The Godfather*, released in 1972, grossing more than $80 million, made it the most financially successful film produced to that date. It's worth noting that *The Godfather* also was regarded as one of the most violent movies of the decade. Two years later another highly violent movie achieved enormous success. It was *Jaws*, the movie whose blanket national release and innovative nationwide advertising campaign are now regarded as having signaled the beginning of the "blockbuster era."[17]

The unhappy side of the blockbuster story is that high-stakes production and distribution also mean that huge amounts of money are often lost. The possibility of blockbuster box-office success led studios to begin spending more in the making of movies. In the early 1970s only a dozen movies cost more than $10 million in production expenses. But by the end of the decade, budgets were permitted to grow with films like *King Kong* (1976) at $24 million and *Apocalypse Now* (1979) at $31 million – both violent movies. A decade later a movie budget would for the first time top $100 million, with the release of *Terminator 2: Judgment Day* (1991). The problem was that not every one of the new ultra-high budget movies achieved success. And when one of these films flopped, its movie studio had to move quickly to cut its losses. In the high-stakes game of national releases and ad campaigns, if a movie didn't prove its potential in the first weekend of release it was taking up space and costing money in hundreds of movie theaters coast-to-coast. The prints of the failing film had to be quickly pulled from theaters so that another potential blockbuster could have a shot at the national audience.[18]

Making matters worse in the 1990s for motion picture companies, the basic production costs of making big-ticket movies began rising at a steady rate. This is due to a kind of one-upmanship on the part of film directors and the growing demand of movie audiences for expensive special-effects-laden films with lots and lots of action – not to mention big-name movie stars like Tom Cruise and Julia Roberts, who command salaries in excess of $20 million per film. By comparison, in the 1960s Hollywood shocked the world by paying Elizabeth Taylor an unheard of sum of $1 million for her title role in the movie *Cleopatra* (1963). By the late 1990s, production expenses for feature films crossed another high-water mark with the release of James Cameron's $200 million movie *Titanic* (1997). But in raising the bar for costs *Titanic* also raised the bar for profits, raking in a record-breaking $600 million in domestic gross sales – an income figure that would reach the unprecedented sum of $1 billion with foreign markets and ancillary income later included.

But the giddy successes of movies like *Titanic* hardly typify the movie industry. Most feature films end up losing money and this doesn't sit well with stockholders in parent companies like General Electric, Time Warner, and Sony. This is why the character of movie making has changed dramatically in the interests of maximizing motion picture profits while minimizing the risks in producing blockbuster properties. Over time the businesspeople that oversee movie companies have recognized certain formulas that tend to work better than others, as well as what kind of movies are more likely to succeed. And that means violence.

A familiar opinion one hears from nervous parents and certain media critics is that there seems to be more violence in entertainment these days. The response often given to these presumably overanxious observers is that it just isn't so – that there has always been violence in movies and in all storytelling. But that answer isn't true. There really is more violence and it's no accident or coincidence. The production and circulation of movies saturated with violent content is part of a newly emerging strategy to maximize the success of the latest generation of blockbuster movie releases. None of this is a big secret. For most of the past 15 years the predominant genres of big-budget Hollywood films have relied heavily on action formats and increasingly sophisticated digital effects. The need to appeal to young adult and teen audiences has caused motion picture companies to focus their blockbuster production on action–adventure genres that once were scorned by the film industry as B-movie and exploitation categories.

Disaster Movies

A study released in 2002 analyzing recent trends in large-budget Hollywood feature film releases documented the dominance of violent action-oriented genres over such categories as family movies, comedies, and dramas.[19] The study found that the largest-grossing film genre in the years 1990–9 was that of disaster movies. Led by the enormously successful *Titanic* (1997), the category also contained such pictures as *Twister* (1996), *White Squall* (1996), *Dante's Peak* (1997), *Volcano* (1997), *Deep Impact* (1998), and *Armageddon* (1998). Such disaster movies have capitalized on recent advances in computer animation, special effects, and sound design to produce immersive renderings of gut-wrenching calamities in which huge environments and what appear to be throngs of people are subjected to the terrifying consequences of earthquakes, hurricanes, tsunamis, tornadoes, floods, fires, and – of course – explosions. In restaging the 1912 sinking of the "World's Greatest Ocean Liner" after it crashed into a North Atlantic iceberg, director James Cameron's *Titanic* proved that masterful movie making (and a compelling love interest in the plot) can draw audiences to a story of which everyone knows the ending.

The recent spate of disaster movies harkens back to an earlier heyday of disaster films. The 1970s witnessed the release of such classics of the disaster genre as *The Poseidon Adventure* (1972), *The Towering Inferno* (1974), *Earthquake* (1974), and *The Swarm* (1978). These movies demonstrated the enormous popular appeal of stories in which ordinary people work together in extraordinary circumstances to form a mutual bond that ultimately results in their survival. In many instances, these struggles bring people together across lines of gender, race, and social class to build camaraderie and find common cause.

The popularity of disaster films has continued in the 2000s, perhaps with good reason. As the international political atmosphere has become increasingly apocalyptic, and occurrences of terrorist attacks since 9/11 move further toward the West, movies are becoming more pessimistic in depicting the possibility of Armageddon.[20] Technically speaking, the long-running "Jurassic Park" series (1993–2006) qualifies for inclusion in the disaster genre in its continuing depiction of dinosaur species reemerging in contemporary times to chomp upon the unlucky people around them, and by extension threatens to eviscerate the entire human race. More typical disaster movies include the 2004 made-for-TV feature film *10.5* about a cataclysmic earthquake. In another big-screen disaster movie made that year, *The Day After Tomorrow* (2004), global warming leads to a new Ice Age as well as massive tornadoes, blizzards, and tidal waves that flood Manhattan. The following year brought the summer blockbuster *Stealth* (2005) in which three Navy pilots struggled heroically to prevent their new flying partner – an artificial intelligence program – from initiating an attack on US soil. Then came movies like *When Worlds Collide* (2006), *The Fly*

(2006), *Resident Evil: Extinction* (2007), and such remakes as *Poseidon* (2006), *King Kong* (2006), *The Texas Chainsaw Massacre: The Beginning* (2006), and *Journey to the Center of the Earth* (2007).

Science Fiction

The success of all of the movies discussed above appears to validate the argument of entertainment industry apologists that audiences really want violent movies. They are not forced upon people or made popular simply on the basis of advertising. Audiences really clamor for violent entertainment, further demonstrated by the next most popular category studied – science fiction. Like disaster movies, recent science fiction films rely heavily on violence and capitalize extensively on special-effects techniques. Topping the list of 1990s sci-fi blockbusters was George Lucas's *Star Wars Episode 1: The Phantom Menace* (1999), the first in his so-called "prequel" movies revisiting the extremely successful "Star Wars" series that had concluded 16 years earlier. Costing $115 million to make, *The Phantom Menace* outdid other films of its kind in its extravagant use of digital-effects technology – accounting for an unprecedented 2,000 shots during the 133-minute film. Other 1990s science fiction films repackaged familiar story concepts such as attacks from outer space or the unintended consequences of scientific exploits gone awry. Many new science fiction films owe a philosophical debt to earlier sci-fi classics of the 1950s like *The Day the Earth Stood Still* (1951) and *Invaders from Mars* (1953). In her essay on 1950s science-fiction movies, "The Imagination of Disaster," Susan Sontag wrote that the genre "is concerned with the aesthetics of destruction, with the peculiar beauties to be found in wreaking havoc, making a mess."[21]

At the time, Sontag suggested that Western society had succumbed to "a mass trauma" over fears that a nuclear war might one day destroy the earth.[22] Such apocalyptic anxieties returned with a vengeance in 1990s sci-fi thrillers. The 1998 film *Armageddon* shows the earth on the verge of destruction as it stands in the path of a giant asteroid, which somehow escaped detection until 18 days before it was expected to hit the planet. In the movie, the world eventually is rescued by a character played by Bruce Willis, who blasts into space with a band of lovable roughnecks who succeed in blowing up the asteroid. Aliens visited Planet Earth in two notable films of this period, *Independence Day* (1995) and *Men in Black* (1997). Bringing comedy to an otherwise somber and hyperviolent genre, *Men in Black* – a story about two super-secret agents (the "Men in Black") who protect the world from an assortment of silly-looking aliens – opened at 5,400 theaters and became Columbia Pictures most successful movie. Other notable science fiction titles of the 1990s include *Total Recall* (1990), *The Matrix* (1999), *Contact* (1997), and the three installments in the "Star Trek" movie series (1991–6).

Science fiction has continued to show its box office viability in the 2000s, with movies like *The Core* (2003). Stretching the limits of believability, *The Core* finds Earth's inner core losing momentum and everything on the planet's surface going haywire. Humanity's only hope is a special new kind of spaceship capable of melting rock that a group of heroic "terranauts" must ride to the center of the earth so that they can detonate a nuclear bomb and get the core spinning properly again. Steven Spielberg's *War of the Worlds* (2005) brought H. G. Wells's classic story of a Martian invasion to the screen once again. Costing $132 million to make, it was one of the most explosively violent sci-fi thrillers in recent memory. Breaking box-office records in its opening over the long July 4, 2005 weekend, the movie raked in $113 million in gross receipts during its first week of release. Similar success met *Slither* (2006), *Superman Returns* (2006) and *When Worlds Collide* (2007).

Horror

People upset about media violence often point to horror films as the worst purveyors of bloody spectacle and senseless gore. And let's be honest, they have a point. Typical horror movies of the *Friday the 13th* (1980) and *Day of the Dead* (1985) variety have a deserved reputation for unoriginal story lines, low production values, and unrelenting sexism. At the same time horror filmmaking – like other movie genres – can yield insights about the public's appetite for violent fare and the kinds of pleasures it receives from such movies. Generally speaking many people like to be frightened by stories – up to a certain point. Horror movies provide experiences that some media violence psychologists believe can trigger conditioned responses. In other words, audiences can experience a thrill of arousal from a vicarious encounter with danger. According to trauma researcher Lenore Terr, "There's a thrill connected with terror in the same way there's a thrill connected with sex."[23] (Of course in many horror movies terror and sex work together.) In the ranking of 1990s motion picture genres, horror movies were the third most popular category. Like disaster and science fiction thrillers, horror movies constitute yet another B-movie genre elevated to blockbuster status when the studios recognized that larger investments in marketing could pay off at the box office.

Horror movies have a long and occasionally noble history, from such early classics as *The Cabinet of Dr. Caligari* (1919) and *The Hunchback of Notre Dame* (1923). And of course, everyone is familiar with such adaptations of famous literary works as *Frankenstein* (1931), *Dracula* (1931), *Dr. Jekyll and Mr. Hyde* (1931), and *The Invisible Man* (1933). In more recent years the horror genre predominantly has followed cycles driven by fads in movie popularity. Successful titles lead to sequels – and more sequels – that follow each other in quick succession. The notorious *Friday the 13th* series yielded nine sequels to the original film between 1981 and 2001, not to mention ancillary titles like *Return to Crystal Lake: The Making of Friday the 13th* (2003). Successful horror titles have inspired imitations, hybrids, and frequent remakes. For example, the Internet Movie Database (IMDb) lists no fewer than 113 movies in the Frankenstein vein, including such memorable titles as *Frankenstein Punk* (1986), *Frankenstein: The College Years* (1991), and *Alvin and the Chipmunks Meet Frankenstein* (1999).[24]

Besides familiar horror themes of monster attack, extraterrestrial invasion, and devil possession, two categories of horror movie have become increasingly important in the past two decades: suspense-thriller films and horror comedies. Alfred Hitchcock was the godfather of the suspense-thriller with such unforgettable directing credits as *Psycho* (1960) and *The Birds* (1963). Both of those movies staged their dramas in banal, everyday environments – a motel and a suburban neighborhood, respectively – turning them into terrifyingly bloody places for their unlucky visitors or inhabitants. Suspense thrillers of the horror genre got a boost in the 1990s with the success of *Silence of the Lambs* (1991), which inspired a new interest in serial killer movies by respected directors like David Fincher's *Se7en* (1995) and Spike Lee's *Summer of Sam* (1999). In the 2000s the outpouring of grizzly movies about real or fictional killers continued with features like the Saw series (2004–6), *The Omen* (2006), and *The Covenant* (2006).

Comedy has seen a big upsurge in horror movies, much to the consternation of many media violence critics. While arguably more disturbing in the context of children's programming, comedy in mainstream horror movies, it is often asserted, trivializes the cruelty and suffering that characters experience, leaving viewers with the impression that violence has occurred without consequence or lasting effect. This line of reasoning leads some in the media violence field to believe that repeated exposure to extreme depictions of brutality desensitizes audiences to violent representations and makes them less concerned about violence in real life. Others contend that audiences of "splatter" classics like *Re-Animator* (1985) and

Brain Damage (1987), as well as more recent examples like *Texas Chainsaw Massacre: The Beginning* (2006), see the movies as funny because of their outrageous excesses of gore.[25] This latter argument certainly holds a certain degree of merit, especially in the context of such obvious spoofs and send-ups of traditional horror movies as *Scary Movie 1* and *2* (2000, 2006). The very titles of these movies and their depiction of serial killers that seem to have been drawn from every other "scary movie" – as well as their obvious parodies of motifs from familiar films like *Scream* (1996) and *I Know What You Did Last Summer* (1997) – clearly reveal the movie's ironic intent. Nevertheless, one is left wondering whether the teenage audience of the *Scary Movie* duo fully gets the joke.

Beyond the Theater and into the Toy Store

If movie violence simply was confined to the suburban multiplex, concerned parents might not have much to worry about. But motion picture blockbusters, as well as smaller films, now penetrate consumer culture in dramatic new ways. Movies are no longer standalone amusements, but components of interrelated product-lines that also include books, music, games, toys, television shows, and the all-important home video market. This is why media violence is driving the people who worry about it crazy. Really popular entertainment brands like Harry Potter and Spider-Man have become ubiquitous. They're everywhere: on cereal boxes, t-shirts, and billboards; in magazines, TV commercials, and fast food franchises. And of course they're in toy stores. The first thing to know is that theatrical screenings of movies are no longer what makes the real money. With the rise of cable, satellite, and home video viewing – a shift that began in the 1980s – the economics of the movie business has changed dramatically. Now home video is where the movie industry makes the bulk of the money on its most lucrative titles. Although profits don't begin to accumulate until four to six months after the theatrical release of a movie, home video has become the largest revenue stream that flows from a motion picture. In fact, home video sales and rentals have become so important for the movie industry that every major studio now has a division to make movies fully conceived and produced for the home video market.

The essential paradigm shift embodied by the home video boom has been the transformation of the cinematic product from something *experienced* by consumers into a commodity *owned* by consumers.[26] The ephemeral product that audiences once could take home only as a memory has taken form as a lunchbox, action figure, or comic book. All of this is part of a larger process taking place across the culture through which people now acquire products as stand-ins for ideas and values that hold significance for them.

To most parents of children under 12 years old, especially parents of boys, the *Star Wars* "light-saber" has become synonymous with the concept of imitated media violence. Every kid has one or has wanted one at some point. And it's no surprise. Many in the entertainment industry will tell you that *Star Wars* rewrote the economics of the movie business. When the first film of the series appeared in 1977 it not only broke all records at the box office in its initial release and in repeat viewings, but it set off an unprecedented frenzy in the retail merchandising market for licensed products. *Star Wars* receives credit for helping to launch several entirely new businesses in the toy and clothing manufacturing sectors, as well as movie tie-ins in the form of books and musical soundtrack albums. Twentieth Century Fox found itself so unprepared for the *Star Wars* craze that it was unable to get the now famous action figures of Luke Skywalker and Darth Vader into stores in time for the Christmas shopping season. But the toys eventually reached their customers and by the time the dust had settled the company had collected over $1 billion in merchandise sales. Within a few years Disney launched an extensive line of products based on its well-established line of characters, an effort that led to the opening of its chain of retail stores in 1987. Warner Brothers began a similar retail store effort shortly thereafter. Licensing of movie characters really took off in the 1990s – that is, until angry parents successfully shut down McDonald's Happy Meal promotion of the 1992 *Batman Returns* sequel. Consumer groups and child advocates became outraged over the violence and sexual content that the fast-food chain was marketing to its core customer base of families with young children. The Happy Meal episode demonstrated just how mercurial a large corporation's commitment to a movie could be, when enough pressure is exerted on the company's bottom line.

But the McDonald's *Batman* controversy hardly stemmed the flow of violent licensed characters into children's culture or the environment of fast-food restaurant chains. During 2001 and 2002 consumers saw the launching of the hugely successful *Lord of the Rings* and *Spider-Man* movies, both of which saturated public consciousness with what in essence were extremely violent stories and characters – and both of which were followed by related movies with significantly higher levels of violence than the original films. According to the Sony Pictures vice-president Al Ovadia, whose company produced the two *Spider-Man* movies, the key consideration in developing a movie-related "franchise" lies in its "long-term merchandising potential and its appeal to more than one generation."[27] Ovadia describes Sony's promotion and merchandizing of *Spider-Man* as a process that began in earnest more than two years before the release of the movie. That's when deals with partners like McDonald's get brokered. It's also when video and computer games start to take form. So that there's plenty to design, produce, and begin their launch in the marketplace *in advance of the movie release.* Movie companies make little or no money on their licensing deals with fast-food chains, but they profit enormously from the visibility that Burger King, McDonald's, and Wendy's provide for upcoming and newly released movies. This is why promotional items seem to disappear from fast-food restaurants shortly after the much-hyped opening weekends of the films.

In a similar fashion, studios like to see their video game, toy, and clothing merchandising tie-ins hitting stores just before movie release dates. The big reason for this is that all of these partners in the selling of a particular "brand" like Spider-Man launch their own independently financed advertising campaigns. As Sony's Ovadia explains, "These deals are all different, but the driving force from the studio's standpoint is media buying, not revenue; it is dollars paid in such tie-in advertising to help advertise the movies, not dollars paid to the studio."[28] In the case of Spider-Man, the partners included Kellogg's, Cingular, Dr. Pepper, Reebock, Hershey's, Carl's Jr., and Hardees, who cumulatively and internationally (along with other companies) launched over 8,000 individual products related to the *Spider-Man* movie. On most of these products, Sony's share was approximately 7 percent, after it divided its earnings with the original owner of the Spider-Man character, Marvel Comics. Kellogg's introduced both a Spider-Man cereal and a new kind of Pop-Tart with special webbed icing. To Ovadia, "The goal was to turn Spider-Man into an event. The studio uses its marketing dollars in telling a story; Kellogg's uses its marketing dollars in building awareness."[29]

Television

Television is the medium of choice for media violence critics. Some observers go so far as to say that the entire history of television policy has, in fact, been a history of debates over violence and sex on television.[30] In part this can be said because TV is a relatively new phenomenon, entering the public realm as a consumer item in the mid-1950s. Almost immediately there were concerns over the possible negative effects the new medium might bring, as television inherited anxieties previously held for dime novels, movies, and radio. By 1961 no less influential a figure than US Federal Communications Commission chairman Newton Minow declared television "a vast wasteland" failing the public interest with its menu of

> Game shows, violence, audience-participation shows, formula comedies about totally unbelievable families, blood and thunder, mayhem, violence, sadism, murder, western bad men, western good men, private eyes, gangsters, more violence and cartoons. And, endlessly, commercials – many screaming, cajoling and offending. And most of all, boredom.[31]

In the decades since the "vast wasteland" speech television has remained a lightning rod for public fears over the effects of media, in large part because television is such a widely seen medium and also because its programming goes directly into people's homes. Theoretically speaking, these fears remain high because of the widely held belief that the messages television conveys enter the viewer's mind without mediation and those audiences – particularly young or otherwise vulnerable audiences – are relatively powerless in warding off the negative effects of these messages. Contesting this view are those who argue that people possess native abilities to contest or alter the meaning of messages as they are received and that these abilities can be strengthened with additional education about the ways a medium like television works. Moreover, the viewing experience of television differs from that of a movie or even a book in that rarely does TV command the complete attention of those watching. Instead, television has become one of several kinds of communication typically taking place as people watch TV together in homes, dorms, or sports bars.

Enhancing critical literacy about television begins with discussing how and why television has come to exist in the first place. The technology that made TV possible had been in existence decades before its wide-scale appearance in the 1950s. But it wasn't until the dramatic growth of the American middle class following World War II and the creation of suburbs that a tremendous demand for home entertainment became apparent. Piggy-backing on people's existing familiarity with radio, television emerged as a kind of "radio with pictures." In fact, television's initial broadcast infrastructure was built on the nation's existing network of radio stations. With the exception of one network developed by a TV set manufacturer (Dumont), the early networks of ABC, CBS, and NBC were owned and operated by radio companies that often simulcast programs on radio and television.

From 1950 to 1955, ownership of local television skyrocketed, affecting other forms of public entertainment available to the public. During this period, many movie theaters closed, as motion pictures competed with television for consumer attention. Ultrahigh Frequency (UHF) channels first appeared in 1952, enabling the creation of many more channels. But it wasn't until a decade later that Congress required the building of TV sets to accommodate both UHF and the earlier VHF (Very High Frequency) signals. The diffusion of cable television technology in the 1970s further enhanced the viability of smaller, newer TV stations. Profits for the "big three" networks (ABC, CBS, and NBC) grew through the mid-1980s. But within a few years new forms of programming delivery – cable, pay-perview, and videocassette technologies – began to cut into the networks' market share. The big three broadcast networks had a 91 percent share of prime-time audiences during the 1979 season. This dropped to 75 percent in the 1987 season, and further to 61 percent in 1994.[32]

Like the motion picture industry, television has undergone major restructuring during the past decade, as all existing networks were acquired by larger parent companies. This change in network ownership has meant a greater emphasis on building audiences (or trying to maintain them) while cutting costs and developing less expensive vehicles – like reality TV shows – for delivering content. In pure economic terms, the most important difference between the television and movie industries lies in what they get paid to do. Motion picture studios still make their money by *selling entertainment to audiences.* Television networks get paid for *selling audiences to advertisers.* For this reason the people who sell television programs are even more sensitive than movie producers to rapidly changing patterns of viewer tastes and preferences. The famous AC/Nielsen Ratings service came into existence to provide to networks and advertisers the ability to determine the size of a viewing audience within hours of a program's broadcast.

The intense interest of program sponsors in the size of television audiences, coupled with the skyrocketing costs of producing splashy, attention-getting TV commercials, has created a highly pressurized economic climate in the commercial television industry. If a time ever existed where innovative or difficult programs were allowed to struggle for attention and occasionally fail, that time is now gone. Today television executives are far less willing to gamble on risky programs or to deviate from proven program formulas. This has resulted in a program menu far less diverse and artistically challenging than the vast wasteland Newton Minow wrote about over four decades ago.

The lack of innovation and diversity in television programming has had a deleterious effect on the volume of violence on television. Anti-violence groups like the American Psychiatric Association assert that today's children see over 200,000 acts of simulated violence on television and they will witness 10,000 murders before they enter college.[33] No one can determine the accuracy of these statistics, but the overwhelming presence of violence on TV can't be disputed.[34] Decades of "content analysis" measuring the frequency of violent acts on the air have shown that violence takes place about six times per hour on most programs and two dozen times per hour on children's shows.[35] Does all of this violent imagery really have a negative effect on anyone? Before addressing that question, it's important to note some of the general biases many people hold about television.

Critical Viewing

Animosity toward television belongs to no single group or ideological persuasion. Famous for their condemnations of TV as a purveyor of moral depravity, conservatives see violence and sexuality in programs as evidence of a broader decline in cultural standards. In this view *MTV, Howard Stern,* and *Desperate Housewives* all contribute to an erosion in the values that bind us together as a society by fostering disrespect for law, religion, and the family. Liberals also see negative values promoted in popular culture, but of a somewhat different type. In that view the same programs mentioned might be seen as conveying damaging attitudes toward women, racial minorities, and humanistic values. Liberals often argue that television programming and advertising excessively promote competition and the accumulation of material possessions. Both sides argue that TV is too violent, and both usually suggest that the way to lessen all of these negative influences lies either in reducing the amount of TV people see or in regulating the kinds of shows broadcasters can air. These worries about TV can be grouped into three broad categories reflecting popular concerns over the *content*, the *viewing activity*, and the *ideology* of television.

Content concerns typically follow the common-sense assumption that audiences, especially "vulnerable" audiences like children and teenagers, will imitate what they see in violent cartoons, slapstick comedies, and police shows. This concern has found a degree of legitimacy in recent instances of untrained teenage viewers known as "backyarders" acting out the antics of televised professional wrestling and often seriously injuring themselves. Young children also commonly imitate *Wiley Coyote* or the *Power Rangers*, causing parents understandable concern. Advocates of unrestricted viewing counter that such attitudes underestimate the critical capabilities of audiences and that measures to restrict viewing or program content inevitably become subjective, arbitrary, and overtly authoritarian.

The viewing activity (or lack of activity) of television has concerned people since the medium's early decades, when TV was labeled "mind candy" and viewers "couch potatoes." The concern is that television distracts viewers from doing healthier things like reading books, playing sports, or interacting socially. Considering the growing amounts of time people now spend in front of computer screens and game consoles, this issue certainly deserves consideration. But people rarely watch television with the type of rapt attention with which they view a movie in a theater. They switch channels, talk to each other, fall asleep, or walk in and out of the room. In short, different viewers respond to movies and television shows differently because they bring to the viewing experience a variety of attitudes, backgrounds, kinds of education, and methods of understanding what they are watching.

Media scholars like John Fiske and Stuart Hall assert that the meaning of a media work resides not so much in the specific film or TV program as in the mind of the viewer. As Fiske writes, meaning is "not produced by the culture industry," it simply is offered for "people to use or reject in the on-going process of producing popular culture."[36] The "reception theory" of writers like Fiske and Hall extends earlier linguistic scholarship of "reader response" theorists like Stanley Fish and Wolfgang Iser. Emerging in the 1970s and 1980s, reader response theory addressed the ability of people reading written works to form interpretations independent of the text. "The act of recognizing literature is not constrained by something in the text, Fish wrote, it emerges from a "decision" made by the reader.[37] The authority of the viewer of media works is strengthened further by the fact that radio and television programs compete for viewers' attention with other elements in the home environment. And as televisions themselves became smaller (and bigger) and cheaper (and more expensive) they found their way into every part of the home, becoming everything from background noise to party entertainment. Moreover, individual TV shows aren't that important either because they compete for our attention with commercials, news updates, and all of the non-program filler that makes up half of a broadcast network schedule.

Finally, people have concerns about the ideologies that television conveys. In seeking the largest possible audience demographics, television reproduces many widely held beliefs and stereotypes. Conventional gender roles, attitudes about power and authority in society, and myths about race, ethnicity, age, social class, and sexual orientation get reinforced in the course of telling stories and selling products. The emphasis on consumption and commercial products is probably what upsets people most, especially parents whose children continually learn about new toys or fads from TV. In recent years, concerns about ideology have extended to television news. Long thought of as a medium of relative objectivity, the existence of bias in reporting has been noted by those on both the left and the right as ongoing stories such as the wars in Afghanistan and Iraq grow increasingly controversial. In part this criticism of TV news derives from a recognition that most television comes from entities owned by a few multinational corporations, whose interests inevitably influence the programs produced.

Dramatic Programs

Most dramatized violence on television takes place in shows about police, lawyers, or physicians – three occupations that generate anxiety for many viewers since their practitioners wield certain kinds of power over "ordinary" people. Police stations, courts, and hospitals also are places that most people only see in moments of distress or crisis. They hold an implicit interest and generate a voyeuristic curiosity before their TV stories even begin. At the time of writing, police and crime shows represent six of the top ten most watched programs on prime-time, led by *CSI: Crime Scene Investigation*, *Without a Trace*, *CSI: Miami*, *Law & Order: Criminal Intent*, *NCIS*, *Cold Case*, and *Law & Order*. Accounting for a combined US audience of 69.7 million viewers, violent crime shows are by far the most lucrative thing going on TV.

Complaints about crime shows go far beyond their violent content, though they usually relate to the violence in some way. First, violence depicted has been stylized and dressed up so that it no longer resembles the kind of violence that actually hurts people in the real world. Rarely is the physical pain and actual extent of a violent injury ever comprehensively depicted. That would take up too much story time and production expense. So like every other narrative element, the violence is codified and reduced to familiar moments like a body rebounding from a gunshot or a blow delivered during a fistfight. These days there's a great deal of interest in shows that use technology to solve crimes. As in old-time detective novels, investigators in programs like *CSI* search for clues to catch the bad guys – but in the 2000s they use digital photography, electron microscopes, and computer databases to get the job done. Instead of finding lead pipes and candlesticks, the *CSI* sleuths examine ground-up bits of broken teeth or rodent feces from under people's fingernails. All of this gives viewers the impression that the forensics they are viewing are more "real" and scientifically precise than anything seen before. Making a spectacle of the crime's aftermath in this way engages viewers with high-tech wizardry, but gives them little actual sense of the violent injury they think they are examining.

The more difficult issue lies in the ethics of violence in crime shows. At their core, these programs lay down principles of what mainstream society considers right and wrong, as codified in the law. They tell stories about violence wrongly committed and the consequences and punishments that follow. They show people using violent means to take short cuts in getting what they want. They show people expressing anger with violence. And they portray situations where society authorizes the commission of violence on its behalf. This is a serious business because the ethics conveyed in crime shows tells people that certain circumstances justify violence. Police sometimes need to use violence to protect people and to apprehend criminals. We also need a military to protect us as a nation. But crime shows also often suggest that ordinary citizens can commit violence when they are threatened or in danger, leading some people to believe that violent behavior is at times natural and acceptable. This is where things get tricky – because perceptions of threats and danger are, after all, subjective.

Just think of all the programs where "rogue cops" or detectives become heroes because they take matters into their own hands and start going after the bad guys on their own terms. Clint Eastwood's quintessential *Dirty Harry* (1971) character inspired an entire approach to crime investigation that said: "You don't assign him to murder cases. You just turn him loose."[38] *Kojak, Columbo, Baretta, Magnum, Nash Bridges, T. J. Hooker, Starsky & Hutch* – none of them played by the rules. In *Hill Street Blues* and *NYPD Blues* considerable dramatic tension came from seeing how far investigators could coerce suspects during interrogation and how many ways detectives could extend the force they were authorized to use in the streets. This is certainly one of the keys to the popularity of *The Shield* and of programs like *Boomtown* and *Robbery Homicide Division*. Viewers identify with the lead characters in these programs and with their decisions – when the going gets tough – to hurt people.

Crime shows also tell audiences what violent people look like and where they are found. Typically this has meant young men of color in cities. But the portrait of violent criminals does more than just replicate racial profiles and urban stereotypes. It reinforces inaccurate negative beliefs about immigrants, the poor, people with mental health problems, and anyone who falls outside conceptions of white, middle-class "normalcy." And this is not simply a matter of public prejudice. These underlying social attitudes get exploited by politicians running for office, reactionary religious leaders, and other figures seeking to influence opinion and public policy. Moreover, these distorted views of people portrayed as "others" to mainstream society perpetuate generalized fears and suspicions that erode social interactions on a more individual level. Based on perceptions of an unknown person's appearance, one might cross to the other side of the street while walking home, or move away while riding on a bus, or choose not to help if the person is injured. In this way, stereotypes about "violent people" weaken the bonds that hold us together as a society.

In recent years these images of presumably violence-prone people have intensified with the fear of terrorism. New forms of racial profiling have emerged and – in a somewhat startling new development – been defended by those who argue that the exceptional threat of terrorist mass murder justifies forms of security and attitudes toward individual privacy once considered unthinkable in a free society. Few would deny that the world now faces a significant crisis. But many in the US now believe the greatest threat to that nation's freedom may be a veiled government "solution" rather than the obvious threat of terror. International terrorism and weapons of mass destruction may call for a wise and strong response, but certain provisions of the infamous Patriot Act bring radical changes that threaten the very foundations of the nation. As Berit Kjos has summarized the situation, some of the changes are structural and are intended to transform aspects of the republic itself. "Others are designed to draw all Americans – young and old from coast to coast – into community consensus groups that would manipulate minds, change values, build a collective world view, and promote a form of solidarity that clashes with all the wise warnings of our founding fathers."[39] Looming over those changes stands an intergovernmental surveillance network put in place by the Homeland Security Act, passed by Congress in 2002. At the time President Bush celebrated the passage of the legislation with these words:

> The United States Congress has taken an historic and bold step forward to protect the American people by passing legislation to create the Department of Homeland Security. This landmark legislation, the most extensive reorganization of the Federal Government since the 1940s, will help our Nation meet the emerging threats of terrorism in the 21st Century.[40]

Reality Television

If terrorism has made the threat of violence seem more plausible to people, reality television has made more mundane types of violence seem "real" in other ways. In economic terms, reality shows now make up so much of the broadcast schedule because they are cheaper to make than programs using scripts, actors, and elaborate production set-ups. The non-violent prototype of today's reality television shows was the 1973 PBS series, *An American Family*, which followed the William C. Loud family in *cinema vérité* fashion for a period of seven months. The 12-episode series challenged conventional views of middle-class family life with its depiction of marital tensions that led to divorce, as well as the revelation that the elder son was gay. MTV's *The Real World* came on the scene in 1992, giving audiences access to "real" people rather than performers playing the parts of real people.

Since then programs like *Survivor*, *Big Brother*, *Fear Factor*, and dozens of other shows have upped the ante by adding elements of physical challenge or the threat of possible violent harm to participants. One of the major attractions of these programs lies in the ability of audiences to relate to the non-actors on the screen and the belief that what viewers are seeing is an unscripted series of events. In actuality, most of what reaches the air on reality TV programs is highly planned, enacted, edited, and frequently fabricated to look like spontaneous and tension-filled action. Viewers forget that reality shows are all entertainment creations in which dialogue and action often need to be made up to create the desired element of drama. Or they pretend to forget. As reality TV programs have gotten more outlandish with entries like *The Bachelor*, *The Apprentice*, and *Paradise Hotel*, savvy viewers relish the realization that the amateur performers on the shows are hamming it up. But a level of intrigue persists nevertheless with the understanding that the performers remain ordinary people like the viewers, who happen to be appearing on TV.

Music Television

Parents hate MTV. Everybody else thinks it's great – or at least an entertaining novelty. A discussion of violence on MTV might start with the title of the first music video shown on MTV in 1981. "Video Killed the Radio Star," which featured, among other things, footage of exploding radios, helped launch a new form of television that blurred the lines between advertising and entertainment. In its early days, MTV mostly showed music videos that at their best provided opportunities for up-and-coming video producers and established directors who wanted to experiment. MTV's combination of music videos, youthful video jockeys, irreverent commentary, promotion of special rock concerts, and news and documentaries about bands and performers established the network's popularity with youthful viewers, and it became a leading promoter of new rock music and rock musicians. But the fact remained that the videos were promotions and MTV was a new form of television that presented advertising as entertainment. This remains perhaps the most troubling aspect of MTV to many people. Although its style has become more sophisticated and politically correct, MTV remains devoted to selling music and anything that can be connected with it.

As in other kinds of merchandising, music videos often draw on sexual content to attract the attention of potential consumers. The sexual content of music videos uses a familiar set of characters and plot lines. Sut Jhally has likened the landscape of music videos to a fantasy "dreamworld" where the norms of femininity are distorted and women are portrayed as subservient.[41] In this dreamworld women greatly outnumber men, attraction is instant, and sex happens all the time. This dreamworld is inextricably linked to the fantasy life of teenage boys. The fantasies these boys have of seeing women in their underwear, looking down women's shirts or up their skirts, and cavorting with several women are played out *ad nauseam* in plotlines and camerawork. Unfortunately these episodes can take a violent turn. And when they do, it's problematic. When rock stars tear off women's bikini tops and pour buckets of beer on them it sends a bad message to young audiences. It tells them that soft-core sexual violence is permissible and normal. It tells them that young women's bodies are playthings for men. Ultimately, it implies that it's okay to break the rules and override the boundaries of acceptable behavior in sexual situations.

TV News

No one can explain why critics of media violence consistently forget to complain about television news. After all, a typical evening news program often contains explicit references to terrorism, war, and such crimes as murder, kidnapping, and child molestation. As discussed earlier in this chapter, the Vietnam War provided a watershed moment in television news coverage of international conflict, but the public appetite for grizzly accounts of violent crime can be dated to the invention of the printing press. In extending the grand traditions of media sensationalism, television news has developed certain characteristics because of its current pressurized need to deliver large audiences to network owners. In this sense television news continues to incorporate both the style and the content of entertainment programming, including dramatic theme music, splashy graphics, and material chosen and edited to create maximum impact for viewers. Driving these tendencies even more is the recognition that network TV news has growing competition from 24-hour cable news providers like CNN, MSNBC, and Fox, as well as online providers that deliver ever-increasing audiences.

To maximize the impact of stories by following the traditional "if it bleeds it leads" dictum of commercial journalism, television news consistently reports violent incidents without their surrounding context. Shooting, bombings, and child abductions appear to take place without reason or cause, creating the impression that random violence is always possible, especially in places like poor neighborhoods or international hotspots. Here the surprise aspect of recent terrorism hasn't helped matters a bit in furthering the impression among viewers that attacks are likely to take place anywhere and at any time. Coverage of terrorism also reflects the way TV news simplifies its stories to make them more quickly accessible by reducing every story of international conflict to a tale of good guys versus bad guys. This is a time-tested method of storytelling that quickly establishes familiar elements from legends and fairy tales that pose a seemingly natural force of good against an evil menace. Regrettably, these stories nearly always suggest that violence is the inevitable means of resolving conflicts. To further heighten the dramatic effect of crime stories, news programs focus on the immediate effects of tragedies on individuals and their grieving families rather than on their broader implications as symptoms of social inequality or psychological pathology. When the long-term consequences of death or injury are discussed, it is only when they have reached a level of public attention in the form of a celebrity trial or a sensationalized search for a missing person.

In recent years slow summertime news cycles have evoked a heightened interest in such stories, especially when they involve photogenic younger white women like Natalee Holloway, Laci Peterson, or Jennifer Wilbanks. The frequency of such stories spiked after the summer of 2002, when an unusually high number of child abductions found their way to the airways, including the kidnapping of nine year-old Amber Hagerton in Arlington, Texas. While the number of serious child abductions (actual kidnappings as opposed to missing child reports) in 2002 remained at about the yearly national average of 100 per year, a larger than usual number of news reports created widespread fear that an abduction epidemic was occurring.[42] This led to the 2002 establishment of the nationally coordinated AMBER (America's Missing: Broadcast Emergency Response) Alert program linking broadcasters and police in an early warning system to find abducted children. President Bush authorized the national AMBER Alert program as part of the PROTECT Act signed in 2003. The law formally established the federal government's role in the AMBER Alert program, appointing the Department of Justice (DOJ) as the agency responsible for coordinating AMBER Alerts. While AMBER Alerts since 2003 have aided in the recovery of many abducted children (more than 80 percent of whom are taken by family members), the system also has helped perpetuate a belief that child abductions occur at rates much higher than their actual occurrence. As one might expect, coverage never contemplates an introspective evaluation of the way news coverage heightens and distorts public understanding of these tragedies or the ways that ethical considerations might temper the approach of TV news.

Children's Programming

Media scholar George Gerbner coined the term "happy violence" to describe the way television depicts episodes of physical aggression. "It's swift, it's thrilling, it's cool, it's effective, it's painless, and it always leads to a happy ending because you have to deliver the audience to the next commercial in a receptive mood."[43] Over the years, Gerbner developed a theory about what he termed the "mean world syndrome." What this means is that if a person inhabits a home where people watch lots of television, that person lives in a meaner world than the next-door neighbor who lives in the same world but watches less television. "The programming reinforces the worst fears and apprehensions and paranoia of people."[44] Another consequence of watching a lot of television, in Gerbner's view, is that one comes to believe that the violence portrayed on television is normal – that everybody does it, and that it's a good way of solving problems. TV also desensitizes audiences to victimization and suffering in that viewers lose the ability to understand the consequences of violence, to empathize, to resist, to protest. And TV can exacerbate people's feelings of insecurity and vulnerability. Some surveys have indicated that the more television people watch, the more they are likely to be afraid to go out on the street in their own community, especially at night. They are afraid of strangers and meeting other people. Ironically, many of these fears of violence come from programs typically considered non-threatening.

The good news is that kids' television has gotten a lot savvier about violence. Saturday-morning schedules no longer feature back-to-back half-hours of *Wiley Coyote*, *Power Rangers*, or such great-granddaddies of kid violence as *Popeye* and *The Three Stooges*. Instead the roster comprises a mix that includes programs like *Kim Possible*, *Blues Clues*, and *Yu-Gi-Oh!*

in which characters help each other with challenges, solve logical problems, or chase each other in playful skirmishing. What's going on here? Wasn't kids' TV always a frenetic mess of endless dueling and mindless pratfalls? Something happened in the late 1990s while no one without kids was paying attention.

As the multinationals took over TV broadcasting they recognized the buying power of baby-boomer parents – and the corporations started using their kids' product lines to make TV shows. When ABC joined the Disney family its network shows became family-friendly. CBS found itself linked to Nickelodeon and its kids' shows got more educational. Then NBC became incorporated with Universal Pictures and acquired that company's list of children's characters. Time Warner, with its own array of ready-made Warner Brothers cartoon characters, decided to go after the youth market with upbeat WB Network programming. Finally Fox came along with 4KidsTV. All of this changed the landscape of children's television dramatically. It didn't mean that violence disappeared from children's television altogether or that its commercial orientation changed all that much. But it meant a major improvement in the overall content and quality of programming. The bottom line stayed the same, however. Marketing remained the name of the game.

Perhaps this is an obvious point, but it's important to keep in mind that throughout history all children's stories, fairy tales, movies, and other media have been created by adults and informed by adult sensibilities. Hence the eternal image of the innocent child, an adult fantasy of carefree days gone by and a life without the burdensome concerns of work, sexuality, and real-life conflicts. This is why the image of the child often comes with idealized notions attached of the nuclear family, happy endings, and neatly resolved stories of virtue versus evil where the handsome princes always win and bad people look like ugly stepmothers or grotesque monsters. At its core, the image of the child is an ideological construction that gets pitted symbolically against all that white bourgeois society fears. Although rarely overtly, childhood and its protection by adults at times get called into the service of what British education scholar David Buckingham has termed a "politics of substitution" through which extremists argue against women in the workplace, gay rights, and violent media.[45]

More damaging, Buckingham asserts, is the way the protection of children can limit adult perceptions of what children can think about and do. Youngsters get cast so much as helpless non-adults that considerations get foreclosed of children's ability to think about themselves as members of a larger society in which they participate and will later contribute. Instead of seeing themselves as future professionals or voters, children are given only one avenue of adult thinking to practice. They are raised to be consumers. The one kind of decision children learn to make from their earliest years is how to choose things to have and buy. And this lesson and its array of consumer choices get driven home endlessly on TV, at the toy store, and by parents relishing their kid's ability to consume with sophistication and taste. The kinds of things children choose to want usually come from a marketplace that reinforces the most conventional views of society, often replicating well-trodden attitudes about gender and behavior. Playing with Easy-Bake Ovens and Barbie dolls, girls receive encouragement to behave like nurturing and compliant women. Meanwhile, Rescue Heroes and GI-Joe tell boys to seek action and combat. Is it any wonder that kindergarten girls so often turn out to be attentive readers and boys distracted brawlers?

Sports on TV

Sports media play a part in the construction of violent masculinity that doesn't need much explaining. The public appetite for violent sports entertainment dates to the Roman era of gladiator spectacles. Forms of football thrived during the days of the Byzantine Empire and boxing first became popular in eighteenth-century Europe. Most of today's team sports play out traditional narratives of dualistic competition in which one side ends up prevailing over the other, bringing with it the satisfaction of a conflict resolved through a victory and a defeat. Audiences revel in the excitement of the contest, but they also identify with the participants. Some college teams carry innocuous identifying nicknames like Angels, Brewers, or Cardinals, while others show more moxie like the Bullets, the Cowboys, or the Gators. Team nicknames launched in the days before ethnic sensitivity have elicited controversy in recent decades, with teams like the Oklahoma Redskins and Seattle Chieftains changing their names to the Crimson Storm and the Redhawks.

Whether or not one believes that violent sports exert a negative influence on contemporary culture, one fact is certain – sports play a major role in the socialization of boys. Many argue that this is a good thing, in that it teaches boys sportsmanship, the importance of teamwork, the reality of competition in later life, and how to be graceful losers as well as winners. But this has often come at the expense of girls, who historically have found themselves excluded from these important lessons and the esteem building that athletics can foster. The systematic exclusion of girls and women from organized team sports led to complaints about their equal treatment in school budgets for boys' sports. This led to court cases and the eventual passage of Title IX by the US Congress calling for equivalent spending for women's athletics in all institutions receiving federal education funding. But the legislation has never sat well with proponents of traditional school athletics and challenges to Title IX continue to surface from time to time.

Violent TV sports also contribute to very real spectator violence, the most extreme examples of which usually occur near the games themselves. It happened in Chicago after the Bulls won, in Denver after the Broncos won, twice in Detroit after the Pistons and the Tigers won, and repeatedly in Los Angeles when the Lakers won their series of NBA championships. In some sports like hockey and football, spontaneous fighting between players and with game officials has become an accepted part of the overall game experience, giving many fans the impression that unlicensed aggression is something to be emulated. While most of these incidents start with players, spectators contribute to what has been described as an epidemic of violence in contemporary sports.[46] Remember that many sports fans get a sense of social identity and self-esteem from a team. Emulating players is a big part of this identification. A little team spirit can quickly escalate into outright hostility toward an opponent and its fans. Most media coverage of sports-related violence doesn't help matters. The language of sports commentary is colored with metaphors of combat and destruction. Television, magazines, newspapers, and radio sensationalize the lives of flamboyant and aggressive players. The relationship between aggressive sporting competition and violent everyday behavior gets confusing for some viewers as a result.

5

But We Can Understand It:
Beyond Polemics in the Media Violence Debate

Producers of media violence often say that they are only answering a public demand. Consumers argue that the entertainment industry is inundating them with mayhem and gore. Yet audiences do seem to enjoy and seek out violent material. The preceding chapter of this book explored the ways that the entertainment industry capitalizes on this demand and justifies its practices. But if one assumes that that is the whole story, and that controlling the industry is the answer to the media violence dilemma, one is taking a very pessimistic view of audiences, their critical abilities, and their capacities for making choices. Such a view relieves individuals and families of any responsibility in the matter and ultimately disempowers them by turning the problem over to greater authorities like the government. This chapter begins by examining the issue of audience demand for violence by looking at two media. The first is book publishing, which media violence critics rarely take to task. The second is computer games, the current object of so much public scrutiny and alarm.

Publishing Violence

Most people think that reading is a virtue and that getting kids to read should be encouraged by almost any means – as long as the stories are somehow "healthy" or part of traditional children's literature. For this reason, little scrutiny has been applied to accepted children's books or the fact that most common fairy tales and well-known stories for youngsters are chock-full of violence and threats of harm. The most important thing to keep in mind when thinking about children's literature is that all of it was not written by children, but by grown-ups. And the adults who conceived, wrote, and canonized the classics of juvenile literature had a variety of motives for creating the tales besides simply entertaining kids, including moral education and metaphorically teaching about the "real" adult world, as well as keeping adults interested in the stories. This is one of the reasons why Grimm's fairy tales often are so decidedly grim in their outcomes. Take this passage from Hansel and Gretel, as the evil old woman

> seized Hansel with her shriveled hand, carried him into a little stable, and locked him in behind a grated door. Scream as he might, it would not help him. Then she went to Gretel, shook her till she awoke, and cried, get up, lazy thing, fetch some water, and cook something good for your brother, he is in the stable outside, and is to be made fat. When he is fat, I will eat him.[1]

Like movies and television, the publishing industry is hardly an independent or heterogeneous enterprise. The vast majority of books and magazines for children and adults come from the same handful of multinational corporations (Time Warner, General Electric, News Corporation, Disney, Viacom, and Bertelsmann). These corporations aren't inherently evil. They simply are driven by shareholder profit motives above any other interest. So they seize upon what parents and kids seem to want and, like the movie industry, these days use their national and international marketing and distribution capabilities to most efficiently sell products. This has led to the same kind of blockbuster mentality and homogenization that characterizes other popular media.

A number of widespread attitudes about children further affect kids' culture and commerce. One is the belief that children are vulnerable, innocent, and incapable of making informed decisions. There are degrees of truth in this relating to evolving cognitive and emotional development. But while adults appropriately guide youngsters through the complexities of making decisions about their nutrition or socializing, they often don't pay as much attention to the way kids develop purchasing preferences. Commercial culture doesn't help matters. It envelops children in a world where every film, TV show, toy store, and fast-food restaurant simultaneously promotes the same franchised superhero or blockbuster movie première. This onslaught of marketing takes place, many child experts argue, as children are formulating their identities as social beings.[2] Before most kids think about community responsibility and citizenship, they already have very entrenched beliefs about the importance of owning the latest toys – ideas that get reinforced by peers and even in school. In many parts of the US and other nations, corporations now own franchises to market food and other products in public schools or they gain advertising privileges by making contributions to schools. Buckling under public pressure late in 2005, the American Beverage Association recommended limiting the availability of soft drinks in schools in light of revelations that US childhood obesity rates had doubled since 1980.[3]

Buying things, the craving for products, and the sense of emptiness that comes from unfulfilled consumer desire has become engrained in children's consciousness from the age of four or three or even younger. Like adults, kids begin to link their sense of identity and self-worth to possessing Spider-Man, Barbie, or Bratz toys. All of their friends sure do. And as they grow, advertising continues to tell them that commodities are the key to personal happiness, friendship, and social inclusion. Parents and care givers unwittingly often conspire in this process through their own consuming practices that children observe in the grocery and department stores, as well as when adults encourage children to choose toys and products – even "healthy" or educational ones. In this way a new generation of consumers is created. How does this play out with a specific brand?

Take everyone's good friend Harry Potter, the most successful product line in human history – a fairly violent one at that. The last two Harry Potter books, *Harry Potter and the Half-Blood Prince* (2005) and *Harry Potter and the Order of the Phoenix* (2003) broke publishing sales records by selling 6.9 million and 5 million copies respectively in the US alone on their first day of publication.[4] They were published by the world's largest publisher of children's books, magazines, videos, and related products – the multi-billion-dollar Scholastic, Inc., which also is responsible for the *Clifford*, *I Spy*, *Magic School Bus*, and *Klutz* lines, as well as licensed products for *Barney*, *Scooby Doo*, *Star Wars*, *Shrek*, and *Shark Tale*, among others. The actual copyright on Harry Potter is owned by its author J. K. Rowling, stridently represented by the mammoth Christopher Little Literary Agency and backed up by their movie and merchandising partner Time Warner.

As its name implies, Scholastic achieves its success in part through its image as an educational entity. The Harry Potter phenomenon flourished as a relatively harmless set of stories that fostered a healthy interest in reading among young people all over the world. The basic story of a good-hearted orphan who gains magical powers to fight evil while frustrating his small-minded aunt and uncle had an obvious appeal to both boys and girls, even though its surface appeal to occult beliefs upset traditional religious followers. Not that Christian fundamentalists have been the only ones to harbor reservations about Harry Potter. Feminists critics, among others, have noted the way the seemingly familiar rags-to-riches adventure story not so subtly gives boys and men the biggest roles as heroes, especially

Harry, his sidekick Ron, father-figure Dumbledore, and evil nemesis Voldemort. Brainy Hermione and stuffy teacher Minerva McGonagall sometimes help save the day, but most other girls and women function in stereotypical roles as supportive partners or inexplicable neurotics.

There is nothing original about Harry Potter. As Jack Zipes writes in *Sticks and Stones: The Disturbing Success of Children's Literature from Slovenly Peter to Harry Potter*, Harry is "David, Tom Thumb, Jack the Giant Killer, Aladdin, and Horatio Alger all in one."[5] The structure of the novels resembles that of a conventional fairy tale: "a modest protagonist, typically male, who does not at first realize how talented he is and who departs from his home or is banished."[6] He enters a magical forest or unknown realm on his quest, meets friends, animals, or a wise sage, acquires assets to help him, and ultimately confronts a monster or opponent that he must fight to accomplish his mission.

> But is Harry really different? He is white, Anglo-Saxon, bright, athletic, and honest. The only mark of difference he bears is a slight lightning-shaped scar on his forehead. Otherwise, he is the classic boy Scout, a little mischievous like Tom Sawyer or one of the Hardy Boys . . . He speaks standard English grammatically, as do all his friends; he is respectful to his elders; and he has perfect manners.[7]

Harry is a perfect model for children who feel overpowered by their parents or other adult authority figures. He escapes from his controlling adoptive family into a world of autonomy and adventure where he always succeeds and gains admiration in everything he does. Not that kids are the only ones who revel in this fantasy. Despite Rowling's assertions that she did not have any particular age group in mind when she began the *Harry Potter* books (the first was released in 1997), her publishers initially targeted them at children between 9 and 15.[8] Nevertheless they have acquired fans of all ages, and the books have more recently been released in two editions, one with the original "children's" cover artwork and one with artwork more consciously aimed at adult readers. Additionally, as the series has developed, Rowling's writing style has become more sophisticated, and the content of the books has matured, as Harry Potter has grown older. For example, romantic relationships are discussed as an issue for the teenage characters in later books. Consequently the reading age for the books has risen as the series has unfolded.

Violence lurks in the background of all of the Harry Potter stories, beginning with the murder of Harry's parents and continuing through his encounters with monsters, assassins, and the evil Voldemort – who thinks nothing of torturing his victims. The series has grown in popularity at a time when people around the world have become increasingly fearful of terrorism, which parallels the menace of Lord Voldemort and his anonymous followers, who like Al Qaeda are portrayed as infiltrating civilized society. In the most recent book, *Harry Potter and the Half-Blood Prince*, Rowling went further than ever in drawing parallels with contemporary world events in depicting an anthrax-like poison delivered through the wizard mail and a government arresting innocent suspects. Set in England, the Harry Potter books project a feud between an evil cult and a group of people who have inherited wizard traits (minorities and others can gain them with study). Until the 2005 book, the Harry Potter series largely reinforced many us-versus-them stereotypes and furthered the perception that the world is seething with inexplicable and invisible dangers. Only in *The Half-Blood Prince* has Rowling begun to humanize the villain Voldemort by explaining his unwanted birth, abused upbringing, and development into a psychopathic being who uses his talents for bad rather than good.

Computer and Video Games

Games are the final frontier in the media violence debate. They now constitute a bigger market than movies and they are only going to get bigger. In the US people now spend over $27 billion per year on video and computer games.[9] While some game producers are subsidiaries of the big entertainment conglomerates, the two largest gaming companies manufacture the major game devices: the Sony PlayStation, Microsoft X-Box, and Nintendo GameQube. A 2005 study showed that 76.2 million people in the United States play videogames, up from 67.5 million a year before, representing an increase of 11.4 percent that reportedly is diminishing the amount of TV that adolescents watch.[10] To many adults video games are a source of bewilderment and anxiety. They conjure up images of pinball machines, arcades, and growing up too quickly. And most are indisputably violent – as well as frequently sexist and racist. Recent revelations that popular games like *Grand Theft Auto: San Andreas* can include hidden explicit sections have alarmed parents and public officials. This territory, once reserved for headline-hungry politicians, has been entered by such mainstream figures on both sides of the political aisle as Senators Hillary Clinton (D-NY), Joe Lieberman (D-CT), Sam Brownback (R-KS), and Rick Santorum (R-PA), who have sponsored legislation to investigate violent games. It should go without saying that practically none of the adult critics of computer and video games has ever played them. But the testimony of "so-called" experts has been sufficient to convince most observers that the interactive character of games is a far more powerful force than the passively consumed media of movies and TV. This argument has been put most powerfully (if simplistically) by David Grossman, a retired military trainer and self-styled "professor of killogogy."[11] In his widely cited book, *Stop Teaching Our Kids to Kill*, Grossman contends that consumer video games resemble the game-like combat simulators used in military training and that the games transform unwitting children into conditioned murderers.

Simplistic as Grossman's arguments might appear, they seem to convince many adults. But if anyone in the military was taking these claims seriously, the government might have stopped the US Army from developing its popular video game, *America's Army*, which it has widely circulated as a promotional tool for several years. In its latest iteration, *America's Army: The Rise of a Soldier* (2005), players assume the role of an infantryman (women soldiers aren't portrayed) who fights, shoots, and blows things up. As the *America's Army* website states, since its launch in 2002, over

> 5.5 million players have registered to join the *America's Army* experience. These players have participated in over 94 million hours of online play exploring Soldiering as members of elite U.S. Army units. These devoted fans catapulted *America's Army* into the top five online action games at its launch and have kept *America's Army* at the top of the charts ever since.[12]

Used primarily as a recruiting tool, *America's Army* is played recreationally by active-duty soldiers who attest to its authenticity. As yet it appears that no one inside or outside the army who has played the game has gotten confused about where the game ends and reality begins. But the game has generated controversy. As one reporter states, "It's one thing if the Army wants to use video games to desensitize soldiers so they can more easily kill 'the enemy.' But it's another thing to desensitize civilians in the same way, especially impressionable young people."[13]

The actual research on video and computer games has been mixed. Studies such as those conducted by J. B. Funk, G. Flores, D. D. Buchman, and J. N. Germann and by Derek Scott failed to prove a link between game playing and increased aggression, although the Funk study noted a higher tendency toward violence among nine-to-eleven-year olds who said they preferred the violent games.[14] A 2001 meta-analysis written by J. L. Sherry found the overall influence of video games to be considerably less than that of television.[15] While the link to aggressive behavior remains tenuous, a variety of papers and studies associate game playing with other deleterious consequences. Green and Asher asserted connections between game playing and hypertension and muscle strain. J. Tevlin found that games made players less attentive to problems in their lives.[16] Ricci and Videvan note connections to seizures.[17] C. A. Phillips, S. Rolls, A. Rouse, and M. D. Griffiths found evidence that gaming was associated with obesity and even a lax approach to school homework.[18] On the other hand scholars like Gregg Costikyan argue that games actually help people improve their problem-solving skills.[19] RD Health has claimed that games foster skills that lead to faster information processing.[20] Beyond Online Limited asserts that game playing can contribute to stress relief and pain management.[21]

At the very least, it reasonably can be asserted that video games entail their own kind of "literacy" – like media literacy – that differs from spoken or written communication and has new and exciting applications beyond the theoretical realm. Some scholars have begun to write in a positive way about the kinds of learning that video games foster. James Gee remarks in his book *What Video Games Have to Teach us about Learning and Literacy* that people assume roles in video games through which they learn about the world from different perspectives.[22] Although the "world" players experience generally is cartoon-like or violent, the experience can be mindtransforming and lead to useful insights, Gee asserts. For one thing, even in simple games players often need to make subtle decisions. In the widely visited Neopets universe, participants as young as four or five years choose up to four "pets" to own, nurture, and protect. Neopets players earn points, feed, and even fight for their pets, but must decide which ones to favor and which to neglect and permit possibly to expire (which also occurs if players ignore them for more than a couple of days).

So which is it? Do video games teach kids to become violent or not? One thing is certain. Computer and video games indeed do teach young people some computer-oriented skills and they draw youngsters into them in the process. Otherwise they wouldn't work. Any casual observer who has tried to play a video game quickly discovers that you can't simply pick up a Sony PlayStation controller and go. A basic PlayStation control module unit itself has 15 buttons and knobs, several of which move in four directions. The buttons change function as you go along, and you need to keep up with the game. Most unpracticed players who pick up a copy of *Halo* or *Grand Theft Auto* lose the first game or "die" in a matter of seconds through simple ineptitude.

In many games players must construct the characters – even in combat games – choosing from different costumes, attributes, and skills. This is especially the case in games like *Everquest* or *Arcanum*, in which players enter fantasy environments inhabited by creatures like elves and gnomes. In the process, players must learn rules, formulate strategies, and make decisions affecting the well-being of others. But it's not as simple as choosing a wand or a hat. In many cases, this means working against menacing forces far more true-to-life than evil wizards. In *Grand Theft Auto: San Andreas* one becomes a former gang member sought by police in an urban locale where to survive one must constantly fight and commit crimes. *Halo 2* is the story of a genetically enhanced supersoldier who is the only person to successfully defy a group of alien races bent on destroying Earth. Games like *Half-Life*, *Deux Ex*, and *Red Faction* pit contestants against powerful rich people or corporations. *Medal of Honor Allied Assaults* portrays World War II and contains scenes of famous confrontations like the battle of Omaha Beach.

As these examples suggest, their role playing requires participants to place themselves in identities far removed from that of a typical suburban 14-year-old. The experience of immersion in an imaginary universe heightens this experience. Some theorists argue that this act of imagining and to some extent experiencing a novel identity helps young people understand human difference and become more sympathetic toward people unlike themselves.[23] This position is countered by observations that shooting at police, urban minorities, or Muslims simply reinforces damaging stereotypes. (An example of the latter problem occurs in the game *Ethnic Cleansing*, where players kill African Americans, Latinos, and Jews.) Another potentially positive attribute of many games lies in the way characters frequently act in teams or mini-communities through which allies support each other and engage other groups.

Electronic games come in a number of media formats – from those sold in stores on CDs or DVDs to those accessed on-line. In some online games players engage friends or acquaintances in the same room or dorm or other limited network. Other games involve huge online communities of thousands of players. One of the leading trends influencing the video game market is portable gaming, which continues to grow strongly. According to a Ziff Davis study, 40 percent of video gamers are likely to purchase a portable gaming device in the next twelve months.[24] Nearly half of video gamers play games on their cell phones.

Many people concerned about media violence worry about the internet as both a source of harmful content and a stalking ground for non-imaginary predators. Generally most parents are more concerned about sexual material and their concern has successfully mobilized industry to work on the problem. Web search engines like Google and Yahoo come automatically set to filter out adult content so that young people can't accidentally call up pornography. (The filters can be adjusted by any user.) Commercial parental control applications like Cybersitter or Net Nanny similarly limit information computers can receive and simplify the process of monitoring what sites the computer accesses. But none of these safety measures do anything about violent content on the internet. Hate groups like Aryan Nations and the Ku Klux Klan have long used the net to convert new recruits. Some white supremacy groups like Stormfront have created separate children's hate sites to entice youngsters. The strength of online hate sites lies in their ability to reach individuals who might be inhibited by fear of social embarrassment from buying printed materials or attending a hate group meeting. As with online pornography, the internet allows people to view hate materials in the privacy of their homes.

Recent controversies about hidden sexual content in video games have refocused discussion on ratings. Like the movie and television industries, the game industry established its own ratings bureau, the Entertainment Software Rating Board (ESRB) in 1994, which successfully headed off legislative efforts to regulate game content. Games are packaged with labels such as "EC" (Early Childhood), "E" (Everyone), "T" (Teen), "M" (Mature), and "AO" (Adult Only). But consumer groups argue that because no legislation exists to enforce the age restrictions on the labels, stores routinely sell adult-oriented games to youngsters. Efforts in the US began late in 2005 to criminalize the sale of adult video games to minors following revelations that *Grand Theft Auto: San Andreas* contained hidden adult scenes that could be revealed with a software key circulating on the internet.

There really is no way to protect people from finding violent imagery and expressions of hate on the internet short of unplugging the computer. But with the anticipated growth of wireless gaming via cell phones and other devices, the plug will become irrelevant as devices become smaller and more portable. Dramatic growth is expected in the video game industry as it continues to shift with the software market to online delivery. As more and more consumers get high-speed internet lines through DSL and satellite services, more entertainment and communication will come to homes through that technology. Less will be bought at the store as stores of many kinds will be replaced by internet ordering and delivery. The video game market is expected to double in Western nations during the next three years and triple in the Asia/Pacific region.

The Desire for Media Violence

When all is said and done the fact remains that media violence is not something done to us by a malevolent force of corporate greed or cultural evil. People want media violence, they enjoy it, and to some extent society needs media violence. Not convinced? Obviously a great deal has been thought and written about this subject, much of it summarized, synthesized, or contested in this book. Whether or not we want to admit it, media violence is a part of our lives and it's here to stay. But we can try to understand it by taking an honest look at how it functions in society. One might choose any of a number of ways to try to understand why we want and even need media violence. These can be addressed in terms of economics, aesthetics, storytelling, ethics, and memory.

The economy of media violence is obvious. Violence is something people want to see and they are willing to pay for it. The curiosity about what violence looks like and what its effects look like is what makes people slow down when driving past automobile accidents. In 1757 Edmund Burke wrote about the pleasure derived from images of suffering, stating "I am convinced we have a degree of delight, and that no small one, in real misfortunes and pains of others."[25] He added, "There is no spectacle we so eagerly pursue, as that of some uncommon and grievous calamity."[26] Susan Sontag explored the cultural underpinnings of this human appetite for the sight of suffering in her 2003 book *Regarding the Pain of Others.*[27] Sontag observed that people liked pictures of violence almost as much as they liked seeing nakedness. It was almost like they wanted to be asked, "Can you look at this?"[28] "There is a satisfaction of being able to look at the image without flinching. Then there is the pleasure of flinching."[29]

The Aesthetics of Violence

People take pleasure in media violence because it is no longer real. The aesthetics of pictures makes it dazzling or even beautiful. Contemporary violent films use an elaborate array of devices that viewers have come to accept as real. Multi-camera cinematography records action from many angles and perspectives, quick-paced montage editing heightens perceptions of fact, movement and excitement, slow-motion segments draw attention into the scene and heighten the illusion of reality, audio effects in the Foley studio and dramatic music stir excitement further. All of this contributes to what Stephen Prince termed a "stylistic rendition of violence." Writing of Sam Peckinpah's stylistic renderings, Prince describes a three-part process of montage construction:

> The relatively simple, slow-motion insert crosscut into the body of a normal-tempo sequence; the synthetic superimposition of multiple lines of action with radical time-space distortions in a montage set-piece; and montages approaching Eisenstein's notion of intellectual editing, wherein the viewer is moved to cognitively grasp psychological or social truths.[30]

Because people want to see violent images, works using violence become commodities. Whether one blames supply or demand, the market for media violence remains intact, vibrant, and growing. People like media violence, often for the wrong reasons. It gets attention quickly and spices up movies, TV shows, and games. It lives in the culture of masculinity, strength, and national strength. Images of suffering can turn into objects separated from the thing itself. People look at the images without seeing the actual pain. This can have a number of effects. Roland Barthes believed that shocking images of human suffering send us the message that horror has already happened and is over. The pictures offer evidence of something the viewer will not experience. "Such images do not compel us to action, but to acceptance. The action has already been taken, and we are not implicated."[31] Put another way, the images tell us that we are safe and that the violence in the picture has been done to someone else – often in a faraway land.

Media violence is made attractive by artists and technicians. Most of what we see isn't real. The audiences won't tell you that because they don't fully want to admit that they know what they are viewing is a contrivance – a make-believe violent explosion, catastrophe, or fight – that serves as a stand-in for the real thing that they cannot bear or do not know. As photographer Alfredo Jarr wrote, the camera never really records the full experience of what one sees.[32] It records an abstraction of the event. In one of society's great ironies, pictures of violence sometimes become regarded as great art. They imbue transcendental meaning, even beauty, and if such images are in short supply they accrue great monetary value to those willing to pay. When violent images are plentiful another irony transpires as they lose meaning in their abundance. Any single story of suffering becomes lost in an ocean of represented suffering. Personal tragedies multiply into a statistical report of losses. Or they are intentionally minimized by the bureaucratic language of casualties or "collateral damage."

Narratives of Violence

Media violence enlivens stories and is a part of stories that need telling. Excitement comes from the anticipation and experience of vicarious violence. It's like salt on food. Everybody likes it even though it's not good for you. The entertainment industry may capitalize on the human appetite for violence, but it doesn't create the hunger. For this reason violence has become an ingredient of fairy tales and fiction writing, most top-grossing movies, and the majority of what we see on TV and what people want in video games. And much of the violence in entertainment that breaks box-office records isn't really that violent after all. It's noise and light and special effects that in a funny way make people comfortable because the representations of violence seem so familiar. Because what audiences really want is the comfort of a familiar story. CBS mega-executive Leslie Moonves said that audiences don't like dark outcomes. "They like story. They do not respond to nervous breakdowns and unhappy episodes that lead nowhere. They like their characters to be part of the action. They like strength, not weakness."[33] They like the excitement in their stories – and media violence provides that excitement.

Some media producers have attempted to turn this taste for violence back upon itself by upsetting the familiar ways violence was portrayed. Avant-garde artists had long theorized that audiences would be shaken out of complacency by radically "new" ways of seeing things. Could a movie shock an audience that much? In the 1960s director Sam Peckenpah made the claim that his movie *The Wild Bunch* (1969) was intended as a statement of protest against the war in Vietnam. In the movie a group of aging US outlaws try to rob a bank in Texas and then escape to Mexico. There they try to steal a shipment of guns for a Mexican general. In the process lots of gun fighting takes place and many, many people get killed. The violence is extremely graphic, so graphic that people viewing the film frequently remarked that it had gone too far in making the bloodshed "real." Prince has written extensively about Peckinpah's movie making and the many innovations that Peckinpah brought to the craft of putting a film together. Prince has made the important point that what Peckinpah achieved was to make viewers believe in the reality of what they were seeing by using a sophisticated combination of techniques and filmmaking tricks. But most importantly, Prince believed that Peckinpah meant what he said about trying to make people feel sympathy for the victims and combatants of war. Peckinpah said:

We watch our wars and see men die, really die, every day on television, but it doesn't seem real. We don't believe those are real people dying on the screen. We've been anesthetized by the media. What I do is show people what it's really like . . . To negate violence it must be shown for what it really is, a horrifying, brutalizing, destructive, ingrained part of humanity.[34]

Peckinpah learned some of what he knew about portraying violence from the films of Akira Kurosawa. In Kurosawa's movies many cameras were used to catch the action from different angles and the footage was cut in short segments to dramatize the action. To add further intensity, Kurosawa would alternate slow-motion and normal-speed footage to jar viewers into paying attention. Kurosawa also would use long telephoto lenses to focus attention on important elements in scenes. With the support of Warner Brothers Studio, Peckinpah was able to take these techniques and make a movie on a scale that Kurosawa could not. Peckinpah brought it all together in the spectacular gunfight massacres in *The Wild Bunch* and audiences went wild over the movie. Many later films were styled on the model that Peckinpah created.

The narrative dramatization of violence sometimes succeeds in news coverage. It helped rally anti-war activism during the Vietnam War and it made the more recent tragedies of the 9/11 terrorist attacks and the 2005 wreckage of hurricane Katrina more real to the US population – a people which once believed it could not be touched by the horrors of war and disaster. The convincing character of news coverage to some has been used as a rationale for suppressing violent imagery. This was the case with the heated debate over footage of kidnapped American journalist Daniel Pearl, who was murdered on camera by his captors in 2002. Subsequent hostage murder videos have been withheld from broadcast out of respect for the victims' families. The emotionalism of victim imagery is what many say is behind the heavy control on news reporting the US has exerted in its Persian Gulf wars since 1991.

The Ethics of Media Violence

Media violence sometimes evokes ethical issues that society needs to address. War reporting can lead to debate and disagreement. Images of conflict can either result in a cry for peace, or evoke calls for revenge. In her classic work *On Violence*, Hannah Arendt pointed out that although violence is often associated with power, the two concepts really are quite independent phenomena.[35] Violence is a tool – like strength, money, or rhetoric – that people use to get or sustain power. And violence is a crude instrument because it so often gets taken over by anticipation of the thing it will achieve. As it turns out, violence often reflects political power less than it reflects a loss of power – as a failing regime or underdog group commits violence to regain authority or stage a *coup*.

Or violence is simply a matter of convenience, a way of speeding up a negotiation between disagreeing parties that would otherwise get bogged down in civil discussion. In this regard democracy is inherently a politics of non-violence because it implies that those involved will submit to the outcome of a vote rather than a clash of forces. One of the moral arguments against the US invasion of Iraq stems from this very issue. Many still ask why a reasoned discussion had to be abandoned in favor of a unilateral attack. At the time the Bush administration argued that more talking would give Iraq the time it needed to build horrible weapons. This created the rationale for a "just war" vindicated by the moral argument that further discussion would lead only to more terrible consequences from anticipated Iraqi aggression resulting from that nation's perceived immorality and irrationality.

Similar justifications for violent action appear everywhere in contemporary culture. They begin in stories for children that imbue nature itself with moral capacity, as nature is anthropomorphized. A wolf becomes evil rather than instinctively predatory. A storm becomes a "killer hurricane" as though it had harmful intentions. This belief among children that natural phenomena can be "good" or "bad" can foster a worldview of virtue versus evil – a simple set of binary oppositions reinforced in movies and TV programs where attractive heroes vanquish scruffy criminals and "right" always trumps "wrong." If only the world was that simple.

Violence and Memory

Media violence helps us remember the terrible things people can do. This is very important at a time when the immediacy and enormous quantity of information people receive tends to drown out anything but the present moment. Newscasts that focus on sensational details of crimes, wars, and disasters rarely can afford the time to provide background or history to stories. Paul Virilio has written of the way the current age of rapid information delivery via the World Wide Web and the sensory overload of cell phones, instant messaging, global positioning satellites, and 500 channels of cable television mean that people forget far more than they can remember.[36] Virilio has argued that the resultant "speed" of transmission and reception is hardly the positive and politically neutral occurrence that most people think it is.

Memory is an important weapon in guarding against the repetition of human failure and atrocity. As Sarajevo was being savaged by bombs and mortar shells in 1994, its residents wanted to be photographed so that the horror of their circumstances would not die with them. During the mass killings in Rwanda the perpetrators of genocide tried to be sure that everyone was wiped out so that no one, not even small children, would survive to tell of the massacres. As Susan Sontag put it, "Remembering is an ethical act, has ethical value in and of itself. Memory is, achingly, the only relation we can have with the dead."[37] This is one of the reasons survivors of the Nazi Holocaust and their families have for decades clung to the history of that terrible chapter in human history. "Heartlessness and amnesia go together," Sontag wrote.[38]

Responding to Media Violence

Media violence is not the enemy. Nor is it a friend. It seems to be everywhere. But because it's everywhere it's hard to pin down. It does a lot of harm but people like it anyway – even kids. We can try to wipe it out. But it's needed for many good reasons. It seems to be something everyone has talked about. Yet surprisingly few people understand it in much depth. We can begin to iron out some of these contradictions by talking about the issue of media violence. We can discuss it with our friends and families. And we can teach about it at school.

Media education is the most direct and effective approach to the media violence dilemma. Learning about media violence and how violent representations function can help minimize any negative consequences they might produce. It's important to note that minimizing the effects of media violence is not the same thing as assuming we can "protect" children and other vulnerable viewers against the effects of "bad" media. No educational program can eliminate problems of media violence or effectively render them invisible by instructing people to close their eyes, turn off TVs, or "just say no." Violent representations are ingrained in our media environment and they need to be understood.

A fundamental media literacy curriculum begins from the standpoint that messages are constructions. Awareness of the choices involved in the making of media violence sensitizes viewers to the subtle shaping forces at work in the choice of hero, conflict, resolution, and consequences depicted. Discussion then turns to the many ways in which forms of communication differ. Violence on television news is different from violence described in newspapers, and the impact of violent music lyrics is different from that of the violence in popular film. Clearly then, there are purposes in making and sharing messages. The purpose of mass media is to sell audiences to advertisers, and violence is a predictable way to guarantee a large audience. From this it's hard for anyone to argue that there is any such thing as pure objectivity.

Messages that depict violence are powerful because they project a societal view, a perspective on how people can (or should) behave, act, or feel. And in doing this media naturalizes violence, making it seem normal. Fortunately, interpretations differ among audiences. A violent scene on television will mean different things to each individual, depending on the age, race, religion, ethnicity, personal experiences, attitudes, and background of the viewer. Critical viewing reveals when violence is unneeded, wrong, or out of place. More restriction on what is available on TV or the internet won't help the situation very much. But more discussions and more consumer choices will. By discussing the various ways we understand, dislike, enjoy, and use media violence, we move the conversation forward.

Notes

Introduction

1   Seymour Feshbach and Robert B. Singer, *Television and Aggression: An Experimental Field Study* (San Francisco: Jossey-Bass, 1971), p. 12.

2   US Senate Committee on the Judiciary, *Children, Violence, and the Media: A Report for Parents and Policy Makers* (September 14, 1999), in Louise I. Gerdes, ed., *Media Violence: Opposing Viewpoints* (San Diego, CA: Greenhaven, 2004).

3   Realvision, *Facts and Figures about our TV Habit*, www.chamisamesa.net/tvoff.html. Accessed June 23, 2006.

4   Ibid.

5   National Television Violence Study, "Executive Summary," *NTVS Brochure* (1998), p. 8; www.ccsp.ucsb.edu/execsum.pdf. Accessed June 23, 2005.

6   Karl Lorenz, *On Aggression* (New York: Harcourt Brace and World, 1963).

7   George Gerbner, Michael Gross, Michael Morgan, Nancy Signorielli, and James Shanahan, "Growing Up with Television: Cultivation Processes," in Jennings Bryant and Dolf Zillmann, eds., *Media Effects: Advances in Theory and Research*, 2nd edn. (Mahwah, NJ: Lawrence Erlbaum Associates, 2002).

8   Entertainment Software Association, *Facts and Research: Game Player Data* (2005), www.theesa.com/facts/gamer_data.php. Accessed June 23, 2006.

9   Media Awareness Network, *The Business of Media Violence*, www.media-awareness.ca/english/issues/violence/business_media_violence.cfm. Accessed June 23, 2006.

10 Entertainment Software Association, *Facts and Research*.

11 Tor Thoresen, "NPD Paints Mixed Picture of Gaming in 2005," *Gamespot News*, January 18, 2006, www.gamespot.com/news/6142571.html. Accessed June 23, 2006.

12 W. James Potter, *On Media Violence* (London: Sage, 1999), p. 8.

13 Kaiser Family Foundation, *Kids and the Media @ The Millennium: A Comprehensive National Analysis of Children's Media Use* (Menlo Park, CA: Kaiser Family Foundation, 1999).

14 Lillian Bensley and Juliet Van Eenwyk, "Video Games and Real Life Aggression: A Review of the Literature," *Journal of Adolescent Health*, 29, no. 4 (2001): 244–57; Mark Griffiths, "Violent Video Games and Aggression: A Review of the Literature," in *Aggression and Violent Behavior*, 4, no. 2 (1999): 203–12.

15 National Center for Missing and Exploited Children, "FAQs and Statistics," www.missingkids.com/. Accessed June 23, 2006.

16 George Gerbner, "Reclaiming our Cultural Mythology," *Ecology of Justice*, 38, Spring (1994), p. 40.

Chapter 1

1 See Harold Schechter, *Savage Pastimes: A Cultural History of Violent Entertainment* (New York: St. Martin's Press, 2005), p. 122.

2 Graham Murdock, "Reservoirs of Dogma: An Archaeology of Popular Anxieties," in Martin Barker and Julia Petley, eds., *Ill Effects: The Media/Violence Debate* (London and New York: Routledge, 1997), p. 152.

3 Ibid., p. 160.

4 Paul Boyer, "Building Character among the Urban Poor," in Ira Colby, ed., *Social Welfare Policy* (Chicago: Dorsey Press, 1989), pp. 113–34.

5 Herbert Spencer, *The Principles of Ethics*, vol. 1 (New York: Appleton & Co., 1904).

6 J. David Slocum, "Introduction: Violence and American Cinema: Notes for an Investigation," in J. David Slocum, ed., *Violence and American Cinema* (New York and London: Routledge, 2001), p. 5.

7 MPPDA, *The Motion Picture Code of 1930* (Hays Code), www.artsreformation.com/a001/hays-code.html. Accessed June 23, 2006.

8 Herbert Blummer, *Movies and Conduct* (New York: Macmillan, 1933), p. 200.

9 Ibid., p. 192.

10 University of California at Santa Barbara, Center for Communication and Social Policy, Volume 3: Executive Summary, *National Television Violence Study (NTVS)*, 1998, www.ccsp.ucsb.edu/execsum.pdf. Accessed June 23, 2006.

11 American Academy of Pediatrics and American Academy of Child and Adolescent Psychiatry, "Media Violence Harms Children," from *American Academy of Pediatrics and the American Academy of Child and Adolescent Psychiatry's Joint Statement on the Impact of Entertainment Violence on Children – Congressional Public Health Summit, July 26, 2000* (New York: Lippincott, Williams, and Wilkins, 2000).

12 Ibid.

13 American Psychological Association, as cited in James D. Torr, ed., *Is Media Violence a Problem?* (San Diego, CA: Greenhaven, 2000), p. 6.

14 Ibid., p. 7.

15 National Center for Missing and Exploited Children, "FAQs and Statistics," www.missingkids.com/. Accessed June 23, 2006.

16 J. J. Pilotta, D. E. Schultz, G. Drenik, and P. Rist, "Simultaneous Media Usage: A Critical Consumer Orientation to Media Planning," *Journal of Consumer Behaviour*, 3, no. 3 (2004): 285–92.

17 The AAP is one of a number of professional organizations that have claimed for years that studies have shown media violence to cause violent behavior. But, as the letter to the AAP says, "correlations between aggressive behavior and preference for violent entertainment do not demonstrate that one causes the other. Laboratory experiments that are designed to test causation rely on substitutes for aggression, some quite far-fetched. Punching Bobo dolls, pushing buzzers, and recognizing 'aggressive words' on a computer screen are all a far cry from real-world aggression." Researchers have also manipulated data to achieve "statistically significant" results. This issue of scientific accuracy is important, say those writing, because the "unending political crusades on this issue, abetted by professional organizations like AAP, have crowded out discussion of proven health dangers to kids, such as child abuse, child poverty, and family violence. This may make our politicians happy, but we should expect more of physicians." Those signing the letter included: Professor Jib Fowles, University of Houston; Professor Henry Giroux, Pennsylvania State University; Professor Jeffrey Goldstein, University of Utrecht, The Netherlands; Professor Robert Horwitz, University of California, San Diego; Professor Henry Jenkins, Massachusetts Institute of Technology; Professor Vivian Sobchack, University of California, Los Angeles; Michael Males, Justice Policy Institute, Center on Juvenile and Criminal Justice; and Richard Rhodes, science historian and Pulitzer Prize laureate. The letter was also signed by Marjorie Heins, director of the Free Expression Policy Project at the National Coalition Against Censorship; Christopher Finan, director of the American Booksellers Foundation for Free Expression; and David Greene, director of the Oakland, California-based First Amendment Project. See "Scholars Ask American Academy of Pediatrics to Reconsider Misstatements about Media Violence," Free Expression Network, December 5, 2001, www.freeexpression.org/newswire/1205_2001.htm. Accessed June 23, 2006.

18 James Gee's *What Video Games Have to Teach Us About Literacy and Learning* (New York: Palgrave, 2003).

19 Steven Johnson, *Everything Bad is Good for You: How Today's Popular Culture is Actually Making us Smarter* (New York: Riverhead, 2005).

20 Harold Schechter, *Savage Pastimes: A Cultural History of Violent Entertainment* (New York: St. Martin's Press, 2005), pp. 119–20.

21 Vicki Goldberg, "Death Takes a Holiday, Sort Of," in Jeffrey H. Goldstein, ed., *Why We Watch: The Attractions of Violent Entertainment* (New York: Oxford University Press, 1998), p. 34.

22 Michel Foucault, *The History of Sexuality. Volume 1: An Introduction* (New York: Vintage, 1980), p. 68.

23 Blummer, *Movies and Conduct*, p. 12.
24 Terry McDermott, "N.W.A. and the Album that Changed the World," *Los Angeles Times Magazine*, April 16, 2002, p. 31.
25 Ibid., p. 32.
26 David Grossman and Gloria DeGaetano, *Stop Teaching Our Kids to Kill* (New York: Random House, 1999).
27 Ibid., p 75.
28 Senator Joseph Lieberman, "Welcome to my On-Line Office," http:// lieberman.senate.gov/. Accessed June 23, 2006.
29 "On the Issues": Senator Joseph Lieberman on Children and Families, www. issues2000.org/2004/Joseph_Lieberman_Families_=_Children.htm. Accessed June 23, 2006.
30 Christian Resource Center, "Pulling the Plug on Media Sex and Violence," www.nisbett.com/child-ent/pulling_the_plug_on_television.htm. June 23, 2006.
31 Benton Foundation, Headlines Extra – Media & Society June 17, 1999, www. benton.org/News/Extra/media061799.html. Accessed June 23, 2006.
32 The "imagebusters" is the term used in Headlines Extra – Media & Society June 17, 1999.
33 "ACLU Sees Political Opportunism, Not Science, in Report Linking Pop Culture and Youth Violence," Wednesday, September 13, 2000, www. freeexpression.org/newswire/0913_2000.htm. Accessed June 23, 2006.
34 Michael Moore, *Bowling for Columbine* (2002).
35 Hillary Clinton, as quoted in Andrew O'Hehir, "The Myth of Media Violence," March 17, 2005, http://dir.salon.com/story/books/feature/2005/ 03/17/media/index.html, p. 1. Accessed July 3, 2006.
36 "On the Issues": Joseph Lieberman on Families and Values, www.issues2000. org/2004/Joseph_Lieberman_Families_=_Children.htm. Source: AP story, *New York Times*, September 13, 2000.
37 Howard Becker, *Outsiders* (New York: Free Press, 1963).
38 US Department of Justice, Bureau of Justice Statistics, National Crime Victimization Survey Violent Crime Trends, 1973–2004, www.ojp.usdoj.gov/ bjs/glance/tables/viortrdtab.htm. Accessed July 3, 2006.
39 CBSNEWS.COM, "U.S. Violent Crime Down Overall," October 25, 2004. Accessed May 15, 2005.
40 US Department of Justice, Office of Justice Programs, Bureau of Justice Statistics. "Homicide rates recently declined to levels last seen in the late 1960's," www.ojp.usdoj.gov/bjs/homicide/hmrt.htm. Accessed June 23, 2006.
41 National Center for Education Statistics, Indicators of School Crime and Safety: 2004 "Key Findings." Accessed June 24, 2006.
42 Steven Pinker, as quoted in O'Hehir, "The Myth of Media Violence," p. 2.
43 *National Television Violence Survey*, "Is Media Violence a Problem?" www. enotes.com/media-violence-problem/. Accessed June 2, 2005.

44 Jonathan L. Freedman, *Media Violence and its Effect on Aggression: Assessing the Scientific Evidence* (Toronto: University of Toronto, 2002), p. 13.

45 Richard Rhodes, "The Media Violence Myth," *New York Times*, Op-Ed page, September 17, 2000; L. Rowell Huesmann and Leonard Eron, "Rhodes is Careening down the Wrong Road," *American Booksellers Foundation for Free Expression*, www.abffe.com/mythresponse.htm. Accessed June 24, 2006.

Chapter 2

1 James Tore, ed., *Is Media Violence a Problem?* (San Diego, CA: Greenhaven, 2002); Martin Barker and Julian Petley, eds., *Ill Effects: The Media Violence Debate* (London and New York: Routledge, 1997); Jib Fowles, *The Case for Television Violence* (Thousand Oaks, CA: Sage, 1999); Jane M. Healy, *Endangered Minds: Why our Children don't Think* (New York: Simon and Schuster: 1999), and Joanne Cantor, *Mommy, I'm Scared: How TV and Movies Frighten Children and What We Can Do to Protect Them* (New York: Harvest, 1998).

2 David Victor Glass, *Introduction to Malthus* (New York: Wiley, 1953).

3 Francis Darwin, ed., *Charles Darwin: Autobiography and Selected Letters* (New York: Dover Publications 1958).

4 Charles Darwin, *The Origin of Species by means of Natural Selection; or, The Preservation of Favored Races in the Struggle for Life* and *The Descent of Man and Selection in Relation to Sex* (New York: The Modern Library, 1936).

5 Dolf Zillmann, *Media Entertainment: The Psychology of Its Appeal* (New York: Lawrence Erlbaum Associates, 2000), p. 186.

6 Ibid., p. 189.

7 Vernon Mark and Frank Ervin, *Violence and the Brain* (New York: Harper and Row, 1970), p. 6.

8 Ken Kesey, *One Flew over the Cuckoo's Nest*, 1975 (New York: Signet, 1963).

9 Hannah Arendt, *On Violence* (New York: Harcourt Brace, 1969).

10 Ibid.

11 Stephen King, as cited in Clark McCauley, "When Screen Violence is Not Attractive," in Jeffrey H. Goldstein, ed., *Why We Watch: The Attractions of Violent Entertainment* (London: Oxford University Press, 1998), p. 147.

12 Jonathan L. Freedman, *Media Violence and its Effect on Aggression: Assessing the Scientific Evidence* (Toronto: University of Toronto, 2002).

13 S. Feshbach and R. Singer, *Television and Aggression: An Experimental Field Study* (San Francisco: Jossey-Bass, 1971); and R. M. Liebert, M. P. Sobol, and E. S. Davidson, "Catharsis or Aggression among Institutionalized Boys: Fact or Artifact?" in G. A. Comstock, E. A. Rubenstein, and J. P. Murray, eds., *Television and Social Behavior. Volume 5: Television's Effects: Further Explorations* (Washington, DC: US Government Printing Office, 2001), pp. 351–8.

14 Nancy Signorielli, *Violence in the Media: A Reference Handbook* (New York: Santa Barbara ABC-CLIO, 2005), pp. 20–1.

15 Richard Slotkin, *Regeneration through Violence: The Mythology of the American Frontier, 1600–1860* (Norman: University of Oklahoma, 1973).

16 René Girard, trans. Yvonne Freccero, *The Scapegoat* (Baltimore: Johns Hopkins University Press, 1986).

17 Dolf Zillmann, "The Psychology of the Appeal of Portrayals of Violence," in Goldstein, *Why We Watch*, p. 216.

18 Bruno Bettelheim, *The Uses of Enchantment: The Meaning and Importance of Fairy Tales* (New York: Knopf, 1976).

19 Maria Tatar, "'Violent Delights' in Children's Literature," in Goldstein, *Why We Watch*, p. 71.

20 David Buckingham, *After the Death of Childhood: Growing Up in the Age of Electronic Media* (Cambridge: Polity, 2000), p. 11.

21 Ibid., p. 72.

22 Michael Zuckerman, *Sensation Seeking: Beyond the Optimal Level of Arousal* (New York: Wiley, 1979).

23 Maria Tatar, "'Violent Delights,'" p. 98.

24 Ibid., p. 99.

25 Leonard Berkowitz, "Some Effects of Observed Aggression," *Journal of Personality and Social Psychology*, 2 (1965): 359–69.

26 Zillmann, "The Psychology of the Appeal of Portrayals of Violence."

27 George Gerbner, Michael Gross, Michael Morgan, Nancy Signorielli, and James Shanahan, "Growing Up with Television: Cultivation Processes," in Jennings Bryant and Dolf Zillmann, eds., *Media Effects: Advances in Theory and Research* (Mahwah, NJ: Lawrence Erlbaum Associates, 2002), p. 47.

28 Ibid., p. 44.

29 O. I. Lovaas, "Effects of Exposure to Symbolic Expression on Aggressive Behaviour, *Child Development*, 32 (1961): 37–44.

30 C. W. Mueller and E. Donnerstein, "Film Induced Arousal and Aggressive Behavior," *Journal of Social Psychology*, 119, no. 1 (1983): pp. 61–7.

31 Freedman, *Media Violence*.

32 All statistics from Freedman, *Media Violence*.

33 Feshbach and Singer, *Television and Aggression*.

34 Leonard D. Eron and L. Rowell Huesmann, *Television and the Aggressive Child: A Cross-National Comparison* (Hillsdale, NJ: Lawrence Erlbaum Associates, 1981).

35 Fowles, *Case for Television Violence*, p. 126.

36 Richard Rhodes, "The Media Violence Myth," *New York Times*, Op-Ed page, September 17, 2000.

37 Ibid.

38 US Senate Committee on the Judiciary, *Children, Violence, and the Media: A Report for Parents and Policy Makers* (September 14, 1999), in Louise I. Gerdes, ed., *Media Violence: Opposing Viewpoints* (San Diego, CA: Greenhaven, 2004), http://commdocs.house.gov/committees/judiciary/. Accessed October 11, 2005.

39 NTVS, *National Television Violence Survey (NTVS)* (Studio City, CA: Mediascope, 1999), www.mediascope.org/index_old.htm. Accessed October 11, 2005.

40 Ibid.

41 Ibid.

42 Freedman, *Media Violence.*

43 *NTVS.*

44 Martin Barker and Julian Petley, eds., *Ill Effects: The Media/Violence Debate* (New York and London: Routledge, 2001, 2nd edn).

45 Ibid., p. 1.

46 Ibid.

47 Jack Valenti, "Statement by Jack Valenti, MPAA President, before the National Commission on the Causes and Prevention of Violence," in Stephen Prince, ed., *Screening Violence* (New Brunswick, NJ: Rutgers University Press, 2000), p. 62.

48 Rhodes, "Media Violence Myth" and Freedman, *Media Violence.*

49 Buckingham, *After the Death of Childhood*; David Gauntlett and Annette Hill, *TV Living: Television, Culture, and Everyday Life* (London and New York: Routledge/British Film Institute, 1999) Henry Giroux, *Stealing Innocence: Youth, Corporate Power, and the Politics of Culture* (New York: St. Martin's Press, 2000); Barry Glassner, *The Culture of Fear: Why Americans are Afraid of the Wrong Things* (New York: Basic Books, 1999); Mike Males, *Scapegoat Generation: America's War on Adolescents* (Monroe, ME: Common Courage Press, 1996); Michael Moore, *Stupid White Men . . . and Other Sorry Excuses for the State of the Nation* (New York: Regan Books, 2001).

50 Carleton Simon, quoted in Richard Maltby, "The Spectacle of Criminality," in J. David Slocum, ed., *Violence and American Cinema* (New York and London: Routledge, 2001), p. 122.

51 Board of Directors, MPPDA's Production Code, 1930.

52 See Peter Lehman, *Masculinity: Bodies, Movies, Culture* (London: British Film Institute, 2001).

53 James Potter, *On Media Violence* (Thousand Oaks, CA: Sage, 1999), p. 4.

54 *NTVS.*

55 Raymond Williams, *Television: Technology and Cultural Form* (London: Fontana, 1974).

56 Prince, *Screening Violence*, p. 29.

Chapter 3

1 George Gerbner, "Reclaiming our Cultural Mythology," *Ecology of Justice*, 38, Spring (1994), p. 40.

2 Barry Glassner, *The Culture of Fear: Why Americans are Afraid of the Wrong Things* (New York: Basic Books, 1999).

3   David L. Altheide, *Creating Fear: News and the Construction of Crisis* (New York: Walter de Gruyter, 2002).

4   Wole Soyinka, *The Climate of Fear: The Quest for Dignity in a Dehumanized World* (New York: Random House, 2004).

5   Corey Robin, *Fear: The History of a Political Idea* (Oxford: Oxford University Press, 2004).

6   Zygmunt Bauman, *In Search of Politics* (Stanford, CA: Stanford University Press, 1999), p. 5.

7   Louis Althusser, "Ideology and Ideological State Apparatuses," in *Lenin and Philosophy and Other Essays* (New York: Monthly Review Press, 1971).

8   Hans Magnus Enzenberger, *Critical Essays* (New York: Continuum, 1982).

9   Juliet B. Schor, *Born To Buy* (New York: Scribner, 2004).

10 David Gauntlett, *Media, Gender, and Identity: An Introduction* (New York: Routledge, 2002), p. 195.

11 Ibid., p. 39.

12 Media Report to Women, "Industry Statistics," www.mediareporttowomen.com/statistics.htm. Accessed April 3, 2006.

13 Susan Faludi, *Backlash: The Undeclared War against American Women* (New York: Crown, 1991).

14 Judith Butler, *Gender Trouble: Feminism and the Subversion of Identity* (New York: Routledge, 1999).

15 Robert Entman and Andrew Rojecki, *The Black Image in the White Mind: Media and Race in America* (Chicago: Chicago University Press, 2000).

16 Lianne McLarty, "Alien/Nation," in Christopher Sharrett, ed., *Mythologies of Violence in Postmodern Media* (Detroit, MI: Wayne State University Press, 1999), pp. 354–5.

17 René Girard, "Mimesis and Violence," in James Williams, ed., *The Girard Reader* (New York: Crossroad, 2001), p. 12.

18 Benedict Anderson, *Imagined Communities: Reflections on the Origin and Spread of Nationalism* (New York: Verso, 1992).

19 Richard Slotkin, as quoted in Barry Keith Grant, "American Psycho/sis: The Pure Products of America Go Crazy," in Sharrett, *Mythologies of Violence*, p. 24.

20 Michael Omi and Howard Winant, *Racial Formation in the U.S.: From the 1960s to the 1980s* (New York: Routledge, 1986).

21 Ibid.

22 Elayne Rapping, "Aliens, Nomads, Mad Dogs," in Sharrett, *Mythologies of Violence*, p. 252.

23 Barbara Whitmer, *The Violence Mythos* (Albany: State University of New York Press, 1997), p. 67.

24 Hugo Adam Bedau and Paul G. Cassell, *Debating the Death Penalty: Should America Have Capital Punishment?* (Oxford: Oxford University Press, 2004).

25 Ibid.

26 Ibid.

27 Ibid.
28 Lori Dorfman and Vincent Schiraldi, "Off Balance: Youth, Race, and Crime in the News," Building Blocks for Youth, http://buildingblocksforyouth. org.
29 Ibid.
30 Ibid.
31 Ibid.
32 Rapping, "Aliens, Nomads, Mad Dogs," p. 268.
33 Ibid.
34 John Lewis Gaddis, "And Now This: Lessons from the Old Era for the New One," in Strobe Talbott and Nayan Chandra, eds., *The Age of Terror: America and the World after September 11* (New York: Basic Books, 2002), p. 11.

Chapter 4

1 Christopher R. Browning, *Nazi Policy, Jewish Workers, German Killers* (Cambridge: Cambridge University Press, 2000).
2 Anthony Hughes, "Plot Summary for Schindler's List" (1993), *Internet Movie Database*, www.imdb.com/title/tt0108052/plotsummary. Accessed June 25, 2006.
3 Stephen Prince, "Graphic Violence and the Cinema," in Stephen Prince, ed., *Screening Violence* (New Brunswick, NJ: Rutgers University Press, 2000), p. 31.
4 Susan Sontag, *Regarding the Pain of Others* (New York: Picador, 2003).
5 Martin Kemp, ed., *The Oxford History of Western Art* (Oxford and New York: Oxford University Press, 2000).
6 Ibid., p. 5.
7 Stella G. Miller, "Roman Paintings and Mosaics," in Kemp, *Oxford History of Western Art*, pp. 52–9.
8 John Goodman, "Pictures and Publics," in Kemp, *Oxford History of Western Art*, pp. 304–39.
9 As quoted in Sontag, *Regarding the Pain of Others*, p. 62.
10 This and other historical details pertaining to the photography of the Crimean War, World War I, and World War II are discussed in greater depth in Sontag, *Regarding the Pain of Others*.
11 "*Life*'s camera gets closer to Spanish war than any camera has ever got before," *Life*, December 12, 1938, p. 28.
12 Sontag, *Regarding the Pain of Others*, p. 57.
13 Ibid., p. 63.
14 Ibid., p. 67.
15 Amy Goodman and David Goodman, "Why Media Ownership Matters," *Seattle Times*, April 3, 2005, http://seattletimes.nwsource.com/html/opinion/ 2002228040_sundaygoodman03.html. Accessed June 25, 2006.

16   Sheldon Hall, "Tall Revenue Features: The Genealogy of the Modern Blockbuster," in Steve Neal, ed., *Genre and Contemporary Hollywood* (London: British Film Institute, 2002), p. 18.

17   Ibid., p. 20.

18   Ibid., p. 22.

19   Tino Balio, "Hollywood Production Trends in the Era of Globalization, 1990–99," in Neal, *Genre and Contemporary Hollywood*, pp. 165–84.

20   John Hartl, "Disaster Films: Back with a Vengeance," MSNBC, June 4, 2004, www.msnbc.msn.com/id/4981198/. Accessed August 4, 2005.

21   Susan Sontag, *Against Interpretation* (New York: Picador, 1966), p. 212.

22   Ibid., p. 218.

23   Lenore Terr, quoted in C. Robb, "Are we Hooked on Media Violence?" *Boston Globe*, July 8, 1991, p. 27.

24   IMDb Name and Title Search: "Frankenstein," *Internet Movie Database*, www.imdb.com/find?q=frankenstein;s=all. Accessed August 5, 2005.

25   Andrew Tudor, "From Paranoia to Postmodern? The Horror Movie in Late Modern Society," in Neal, *Genre and Contemporary Hollywood*, pp. 104–16.

26   Jason E. Squire, "Introduction," in Jason E. Squire, ed., *The Movie Business Book* (New York: Simon and Schuster, 2004), p. 3.

27   Al Ovadia, "Consumer Products," in *The Movie Business Book*, p. 448.

28   Ibid., p. 454.

29   Ibid., p. 455.

30   Toby Miller, ed., *Television Studies* (London: British Film Institute, 2002).

31   Newton Minow, Address to the National Association of Broadcasters on May 9, 1961. For an edited version, see "'Vast Wasteland' Speech Holds True after all These Years," *Chicago Tribune*, April 24, 2001, p. 17; www.janda.org/b20/News%20articles/vastwastland.htm. Accessed July 1, 2006.

32   "Brief History of the Television Industry," John W. Hartman Center for Sales, Advertising, and Marketing History, http://scriptorium.lib.duke.edu/adaccess/tv-history.html. Accessed June 25, 2006.

33   US Senate Committee on the Judiciary, *Children, Violence, and the Media: A Report for Parents and Policy Makers* (September 14, 1999), in Louise I. Gerdes, ed., *Media Violence: Opposing Viewpoints* (San Diego, CA: Greenhaven, 2004), p. 20.

34   National Television Violence Study, *Technical Reports*, 3 vols. (Thousand Oaks, CA: Sage 1994–8), pp. 1996–9.

35   Michael Morgan, "Violence and Effects Research," in Miller, *Television Studies*, p. 11.

36   John Fiske, *Understanding Popular Culture* (London: Unwin Hyman, 1989), p. 24.

37   See Stanley Fish, *Is there a Text in this Class? The Authority of Interpretative Communities* (Cambridge, MA: Harvard University Press, 1980), p. 11.

38   "Dirty Harry," Internet Movie Database, www.imdb.com/title/tt0066999/. Accessed June 25, 2006.

39 Berit Kjos, "Homeland Security and the Transformation of America," February 2003, www.crossroad.to/articles2/2003/homeland.htm. Accessed June 25, 2006.

40 "President Hails Passage of Homeland Security Department," www.dhs.gov/dhspublic/display?theme=44&content=136. Accessed August 15, 2005.

41 Sut Jhally, *Dreamworlds II: Desire, Sex, and Power in Music Video* (video) (Educational Video Foundation, 1995).

42 Andrea J. Sedlak, D. Finkelhor, H. Hammer, and D. J. Schultz, "National Estimates of Missing Children: An Overview," NISMART: National Incidence Studies of Missing, Abducted, Runaway, and Thrownaway Children Series (US Department of Justice, October 2002), www.missingkids.com/en_US/documents/nismart2_overview.pdf, p. 1. Accessed August 18, 2005.

43 George Gerbner, "Reclaiming Our Cultural Mythology: Television's Global Marketing Strategy," *Ecology of Justice*, 40, Spring (1994), p. 40.

44 Ibid.

45 David Buckingham, *After the Death of Childhood: Growing Up in the Age of Electronic Media* (Cambridge: Polity, 2000), p. 11.

46 Ismat Abdal-Haqq, "Violence in Sports," *ERIC Digest* 1–89 (Washington, DC: ERIC Clearinghouse on Teacher Education, 1989), p. 1.

Chapter 5

1 The Brothers Grimm, trans. Margaret Hunt, "Hansel and Gretel," *Grimm's Fairy Tales*, Universal Library, Carnegie Mellon University (1999–2005), www.cs.cmu.edu/~spok/grimmtmp/012.txt. Accessed August 29, 2005.

2 See David Buckingham, *After the Death of Childhood: Growing Up in the Age of Electronic Media* (Cambridge: Polity 2000).

3 Rachel La Corte, "Trade Group Urges Less Soda in Schools," *Associated Press*, August 17, 2005.

4 J. K. Rowling, *Harry Potter and the Half-Blood Prince* (New York: Scholastic, 2005) and *Harry Potter and the Order of the Phoenix* (New York: Scholastic, 2003).

5 Jack Zipes, *Sticks and Stones: The Disturbing Success of Children's Literature from Slovenly Peter to Harry Potter* (New York: Routledge, 2000), p. 177.

6 Ibid.

7 Ibid., pp. 178–9.

8 "Harry Potter," Wikipedia, http://en.wikipedia.org/wiki/Harry_Potter. Accessed June 25, 2006.

9 Plunkett Research Ltd., "Entertainment & Media Industry Overview," *Entertainment and Media Industry Statistics*, www.plunkettresearch.com. Accessed June 25, 2006.

10 "Ziff Davis Video Game Survey: Gamers Continue to Cut TV Viewing," press release, Ziff Davis Media, August 9, 2005.

11 David Grossman and Gloria DeGaetano, *Stop Teaching our Kids to Kill* (New York: Random House, 1999).

12 "Letter from Leadership," *America's Army: The Official US Army Game*, www.americasarmy.com/intel/anniversary.php. Accessed June 25, 2006.

13 Brad Bushman, "Army Video Game Breeds Violence with Tax Money," *Detroit News*, May 9, 2004, www.topplebush.com/oped376.shtml. Accessed June 25, 2006.

14 Jeanne B. Funk, Geysa Flores, Debra D. Buchman, and Julie N. Germann, "Rating Electronic Games: Violence in the Eye of the Beholder," *Youth and Society*, 30, no. 3 (1999): 283–312; Derek Scott, "The Effect of Video Games on Aggression," *Journal of Psychology*, 129 (1995): 121–32.

15 J. L. Sherry, "The Effects of Video Games on Aggression: A Meta Analysis," *Human Communications Research*, 27 (2001): 409–31.

16 J. Tevlin, "Joy Sick: Games can be an Addiction," in R. Espejo, ed., *Video Games* (San Diego, CA: Greenhaven, 2003), pp. 50–60.

17 S. Ricci and A. Vigevano, "The Effect of Video-Game Software in Video Game Epilepsy," *Epilepsia*, 40 (1999): 31–47.

18 C. A. Phillips, S. Rolls, A. Rouse, and M. D. Griffiths, "Home Video Game Playing in School Children: A Study of Incidence and Patterns of Play," *Journal of Adolescence*, 18 (1995): 687–91.

19 Gregg Costikyan, "The Problem of Video Game Violence is Exaggerated," in Espejo, *Video Games*, pp. 27–34.

20 Cynthia Dermody, "Virtual Relief," from *Reader's Digest*, July, 2006, www.rd.com/content/openContent.do?contented=27535. Accessed July 1, 2006.

21 Beyond Online Limited, "Video Games Can be Used for Therapeutic Purposes," in Espejo, *Video Games*, pp. 65–8.

22 James Gee, *What Video Games Have to Teach us about Learning and Literacy* (New York: Palgrave, 2003).

23 Ibid., p. 151.

24 "Ziff Davis Video Game Survey."

25 Quoted in Susan Sontag, *Regarding the Pain of Others* (New York: Picador, 2003), p. 97.

26 Ibid.

27 Ibid.

28 Ibid., p. 41.

29 Ibid.

30 Stephen Prince, ed., *Screening Violence* (New Brunswick, NJ: Rutgers, 2000), p. 187.

31 David Levi Strauss, *Between the Eyes: Essays on Photography and Politics* (New York: Aperture, 2003), p. 81.

32 Quoted ibid., p. 91.

33 Quoted in Lynn Hirschberg, "Giving them what they Want," *New York Times Magazine*, September 4, 2005, p. 32.

34 Sam Peckinpah, quoted in Stephen Prince, "The Aesthetic of Slow-Motion Violence in the Films of Sam Peckinpah," in Prince, *Screening Violence*, p. 176.

35 Hannah Arendt, *On Violence* (New York: Harcourt Brace, 1970), p. 4.

36 Paul Virilio, *Speed and Politics* (New York: Semiotext(e), 1986).

37 Sontag, *Regarding the Pain of Others*, p. 174.

38 Ibid.

Index

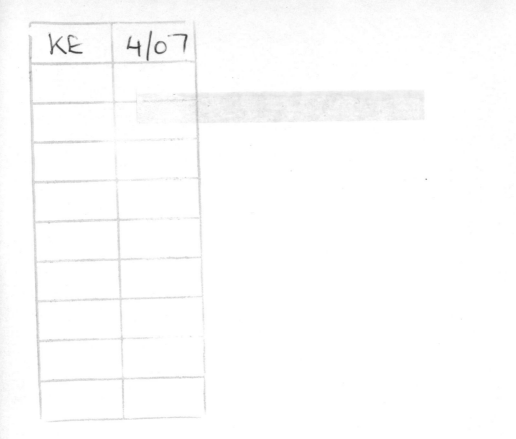